The Next Great Migration

The beginning of how in the Anthropocene

Dedication

The cultural state of humanity is such at this moment in history, that only an informed outsider to the species may be able to offer a view point from an Anthropocene perspective, a view point that may be of value to humanity, as none of the principal organizing institutions of civilization have been able to enact significant corrective measures, lacking the adequate cultural instruments, which unfortunately had not been discovered; that is until now.

It is with that thought in mind that I dedicate this book to:

My family, for their patience to the austerity of family time and economic resources and how else they where affected by my devotion to the work that gives this book substance and meaning. To all of my friends whom for decades supported my devotion to a cause that was never clear to anyone, but that they trusted to be honest and sincere. To all of the Artist Ambassadors of the Worldwide Peace Marker Project collective and its curator Beth Carter bell, without whom this book would lack a proof for one of its central propositions. To Bethy who made the book possible and my personal life of late, joyful and dignified. To Brentley, who without his assistance and loyalty of nearly three decades, the experimental field works that gave rise to Data-A would have been possible. To Mr. Richard P. Bell whose patronage has ensured a place to teach and to create the first examples of Anthropocene art.

Tiité Baquero

The Next Great Migration

Contents

Prologue

Chapter I – Migration is a human tradition

Chapter II – The Holocene Landscape

Chapter III – Humanity's report card

Chapter IV – Welcome to the Anthropocene epoch

Chapter V – CEGE the great Anthropocene menace

Chapter VI – Data-A – an Anthropocene aesthetic

Chapter VII – A culture of peace

Chapter VIII – Modeling a Global culture of world peace

Chapter IX – The Worldwide Peace Marker collective

Chapter X – Data-A and Cultural evolution

Chapter XI – The new great migration

Prologue

There is perhaps no greater joy than the joy of being alive and of having the opportunity to contribute in some way to the preservation and continuation of life in the only place that we know there is life like ours, Earth.

This book is about life and about how we may go about fulfilling the need to embrace a deeper connection between humanity and the natural world, a connection that gets more complicated as civilization and its culture places more and more demands on both survival strategies.

What I mean is, that within civilization, seven billion people struggle to make a living from an unsustainable survival strategy, outside of civilization in the remnants of Nature, some 8.7 million other species struggle with extinction in ever shrinking ecosystems that are under siege by the constant pressure of human expansion.

This book therefore, is not about awareness that there is a problem, or an effort to present an inventory of the critical issues affecting civilization and the general biosphere, or another reference source to scientific research and their findings, or a clever expose of who or what is responsible for the earth's sad state of affairs and much less an effort to incite rebellion against the people and institutional forces presiding over the march of civilization toward extinction.

What ever our species has done, it has done so in innocence of the short and long-term effects of an incomplete survival strategy. These are effects that came as a result of our isolation from Nature and our independent activity, an activity whose incremental cultural growth and focus was placed on the acquisition of wealth and power through force and a relentless focus on the conquest of nature at all cost.

In that sense an incomplete survival strategy means that, we have arrived at a point in our history and development, where the sum total of all of our human cultural context can be seen as insufficient to deliver a civilization that is sustainable, that has managed to learn to live in peace with one another or that is up to date in the caring and upkeep of its own people or of the natural biosphere in which its life and future depends.

That assessment does not come from a capricious observer who wishes to make an uniformed appraisal of the state of the world, rather, it is a statement that is informed by the presence of a new geological epoch of our own making in which the environmental conditions and the prospects for life, based upon the state of the earth's biosphere, which is itself a blatant affirmation of our incompleteness as a species. Add to that the pitiful response to those challenges so far, and we have what amounts to a revelation of the fact, that we do not have the cultural instruments needed to react to the new world intelligently or worst, not in time.

This book is an outsider's narrative of a vision to find a better way forward for the world and about what resulted from following a trail of premonitions that where informed, by the histories of the world, of our species, of civilization and of the forward march of its scientific and technological progress.

Moreover, and perhaps more important, this narrative owes a great deal to the many inspiring masters who pointed my attention to Nature as a source of first hand information and the sciences as a somewhat parallel source of interpretation that has a lot to learn from Nature but that continues to deepen our understanding of it.

I'm also indebted to many of the great mystics whose inspired vision never relented in the pursuit of the mystical quality that surely exists within us, within the natural world and throughout the entire universe. I'm convinced that our perception of the mystical quality of existence will become far more acute, once the reconciliation between humanity and the world becomes an on going active part of human culture.

As I mentioned before, I'm taking the outsider's position in this book because that position illustrates better the narrative that I'm trying to convey. Allow me to explain...

Ideas and information are only as good as they fit our closest and more recent description of the world so as to provide us with a better understanding of what those ideas and information are trying to convey.

As I write these words, humanity literally exists in the transitional period between two geological epochs. That is happening because our description of the geological period known as the Holocene epoch which covers the last 11,700 years, has changed dramatically, making it necessary that we name a new epoch that would describe the changes better. That new geological period is called the Anthropocene epoch and it is named that way for a very good reason, as Anthropocene means "of our own making" the story goes that in the Holocene we began the project of changing the world and the Anthropocene shows the results of the changes we have made so far.

Whatever your take on that, the reality is that we are talking about two different worlds. While the former was wild, plentiful and accommodating to life, the latter is not; we made a new world at the expense of life and the changes we made are so severe and radical that unless we redirect our activity towards life, our world will not be able to sustain life like ours.

That is why I take the outsider's position or more precisely the Anthropocene perspective for my narrative. Like it or not we are in a different world and whatever we do is dictated by the conditions of that world.

While it is true that we are in the new Anthropocene world, human culture remains a Holocene culture which is why there is so much confusion as to what to do and why close observers of the changed new world are beginning to admit that the confusion is largely due to the realization that we do not have the cultural instruments needed to navigate this new world.

Therefore, the Anthropocene perspective is to my mind, better suited to explore this challenging new world for many reasons, most prominent amongst is that the narrative acts or functions more as a guide as we move forwards in a new world than as commentary on why it is important to do so.

The title of the book "The New Great Migration" makes, I think, that consideration clear and if it suggests that I'm the guide, well that would be true also, as the last three decades of my life where devoted exclusively to thinking and exploring the new world, beginning at the same time that Eugene F. Stoermer gave it the name of Anthropocene in the 1980's and later made popular by Paul Crutzen in the year 2000.

I must point out that although the term Anthropocene has not been adopted formally within the official nomenclature of the geological field of study, the world it describes by whatever name has already been with us for a long time.

So, in the following pages I will endeavor to suggest that we, humanity, are already at the junction of either a spiral down to extinction or at the beginning of a great new migration, not a physical take your belongings and travel into a new world that is already here, but rather, a migration of the human mind towards its next highest expression.

Imagine the entire Homo sapiens species migrating towards a unity between itself the world and a new chapter in human consciousness from which the remnants of the natural world can reconstitute a survival strategy for life on earth, that has our hand in its making. Furthermore, that has our understanding in the direction that life will take in our mutual ascent to what we may call the High Anthropocene period. A possible time of stability for all life on Earth and the breeding grounds of what would perhaps become a new species of human in centuries to come, a human fully integrated with the world; "Homo sapiens integralis."

"The Habit of Migration"

Chapter I

Migration is a human tradition

One of the hallmarks of human identity is its disconnect with nature at the beginning of the human project and its subsequent disconnect with members of the same species across the ages, as individuals groups went on to create their own cultural traits an gradually abandoned the history, relation or connection with their common ancestral predecessors throughout the entire history of the species.

That point is strengthened by the fairly recent observation that, the study of the human past and its recent history, has yielded the fact, that our species is African in origin and that we are all descendants form a common ancestor.

While I'm not by any means a scholar in Anthropology, I'm however in awe of the amount of relevant text that is out there for further and detailed inquiry into the very remarkable history of the human species.

Unfortunately, the history itself, also suffers from ideological disconnects between groups whose cultural context, aggressively protects one history to be the one and only and in doing so fail to realize that all of the histories are, in a very real sense, our true history and more importantly that each and every history is a precious part of our overall history as a species.

For the purpose of my narrative however, and in the interest of brevity, I wish to make the point that withstanding all of our known histories and even the histories of their mutual disconnect, migration is a human tradition that goes back to the beginning of our species by whatever history illustrates such beginning.

Undeniably, our world is populated by human kind and at present, we number seven billion creatures whose present location and history is all the proof that is needed to make the migration point sufficient for our purpose here.

It is also safe to assume that we have populated all of the places where we and our technological advantage can make living possible and from that, one can assume that the physical migration of our kind does not have that many new places to go to and migration itself is relegated to moving from one populated area to another.

The migration that I wish to talk about is a kind of migration that we have never knowingly undertaken before and I'm not talking about space travel to another planet. While that idea at present is being proposed by many Holocene visionaries to be our best bet, it is thought about, as a back up, once we are finished destroying planet Earth and is time we move on to begin to destroy the next nearest world.

Despite my flipping tone, it is hard not to think of that as a nauseating notion that while it will be an accomplishment for human science and technology, it doesn't stand very tall as a measure of our responsibility for a planet that we are deliberatively destroying wholesale, only to send a few people into space to carry on the tradition in another unsuspecting world.

Space travel is a wonderful objective, but not as a cop-out for not evolving culturally to restore our home planet and to learn about life like ours before it is all gone.

Anyhow, migration is something that we are very familiar with because the urge is still alive as demonstrated by our space travel aspirations. That migrating urge was amply manifested by our first migration out of Africa about 60,000 years, after some 140,000 years of habitation there.

While we may never know all of the reasons for the migration impulse, we can ascertain that severe climatic changes impacted the environmental conditions favorable to life, thereby changing dramatically the survival odds for our ancestors, making migration a matter of life or death. If the picture of severe climatic changes is becoming a hint of where I'm going with this narrative, you are now in a front row seat to the unfolding dialog.

It follows that once out of Africa 60,000 years ago we spread across the planet and somewhere around 14,000 years ago we made it all the way to the tip of South America. So far so good, fast-forward to 11,700 years ago and the Holocene epoch became the geological wave that we where to ride to this geological junction with the start of the Anthropocene epoch and our presence in it.

But, what does our presence at this moment of history has to say about the state of our migration from Africa so far?

Well, for one it says that we are good at migrating and that in the interim of 60,000 years we populated the entire planet and in the process we transformed ourselves to suit the demands of each of the environments that we reached and settled, that is, until the start of the Holocene when we began in earnest to make demands from the environment to suit the needs of our own developing culture.

At present however, the needs of our developing culture steeply overwhelm the capacity of the Earth's environment to sustain those demands for long and the environment itself is collapsing from the effect of our activity and the way we use the world's natural resources.

Therefore it is emphatically clear that these pressures are at work now, in a similar way as they might have been 60,000 years ago and that these environmental and social pressures are prompting us, humanity, to embrace a survival stand to either transition to a new worldview, which is the only choice at present since there are no new continents open for migration and settlement or to accept extinction by continuing to do the same.

Based on the work that I have done over the past thirty-five years, I believe that there is a form of migration open to us and I'm also optimistic that we can undertake that migration journey because as we will see, a number of the tools that are needed to navigate the Anthropocene epoch are already available.

The migration that I'm talking about is a migration of the human mind, from its present state of development and out of its confinement to cognitive boundaries, which have not changed in at least 50,000 years.

A fact that can be demonstrated by the adoption of a child from the primitive San peoples of South Africa who are known to be one of the few remaining ancestral extant population clusters from which all modern humans descend. That child straight from the San village may be brought up in a major city, learn the local language and achieve higher education at a par with any western child born to civilization.

The end of the Holocene epoch also marks the current outer most boundary of our cognitive capacity to understand the world. In fact the state of civilization, the state of the world and the survival predicament that we are in, is itself positive proof of our incomplete understanding of the world. It is also a survival predicament where our cultural inability to stop ourselves from destroying the world provides ample evidence of the cognitive wall that prevents us from doing so.

This new migration is a journey into a world of our own making, the world of the Anthropocene epoch, a world in which our Holocene cultural context will have to be tempered and upgraded by a number of true Anthropocene cultural additions, adaptations and improvements.

Those improvements are of course geared to increase over time, our cognitive capacity, that is, a sharpening of our faculty of knowing, perceiving, recognizing, reasoning and imagining, to enable us to embrace a whole new level of being that corresponds with the task and the conditions in the Anthropocene epoch.

Later on in this book we will come across specifics about these Anthropocene cultural adaptations, but, for the moment I wish to keep to the migration initiative, those details where mentioned simply because we have to understand that this migration is a real transition from who we are at present, the survival predicament we are in and who we could become in this new and inescapable world in which we have to learn to be a part of or perish.

On that respect, we are not too different from our ancestors at the beginning of the migration out of Africa or their subsequent movements to other parts of the world. What we have to keep steadily in mind is the fact that wherever they went there was an environment hospitable to life, whoever difficult its demands where on the new comers.

The contrast to our new migration is that all of the Earth environment is becoming more and more hostile to life and that what we are doing in fact is, migrating from a cultural context that generated that problem to a cultural context that is capable of mitigating the effects and preside over the recovery of the general biosphere, to again, this time in partnership with nature sustain a world that is hospitable to life forms like us.

Therefore our new migration is principally a cultural migration from a Holocene cultural context to an Anthropocene cultural context. It is also a migration from a largely local and narrow frame of mind to a global and universal frame of mind, from a fragmented and isolated species from Nature, to a species unified with itself and the world.

I need not detail the initial landscape of ideas from which we are setting off, but it will suffice to mention that it is a noisy cacophony of cultural manifestations, which have also taken a hit against that cognitive boundary that I spoke about previously. However, we will be setting off on our journey at the same time, as the sixth mass extinction event in the planet's history is also on its way.

Fortunately we are a migrating species we have done it before and there is no reason we cannot do it again.

We will pack up, our cultural heritage and all of our histories as if it where a priceless cultural quilt that took many a millennia to put together and onto which, we may add the new cultural panels that will enable us to see our new unfolding history as the history of a very complex and unique species whose ability to migrate may very well take on at this time, a survival challenge which can lead it not to a new and distant land, but to the beginning of a new species living in a new and marvelous world.

"The Burden of War"

Chapter II
The Holocene Landscape

According to science, the Holocene (meaning entirely recent) is a geological epoch that on the surface is considered as a rather pleasant epoch with a rather warm interglacial climate that is occurring within the current ice age, according to MIS 1 (Marine isotope stage – timescale) measurements. The Holocene follows the Pleistocene epoch and both epochs are a part of the period known as the Quaternary.

One of the interesting parts regarding the Quaternary period to this narrative is that it comprises some 2.6 million years and that it is a period of time in which human presence or human existence is recognizable throughout that span of time.

While these are vital geological markers in our understanding of the development and history of our planet, they also have a critical role in the narrative of this book because these markers also represent the original natural canvas upon which humanity has painted some of the most beautiful and most terrifying episodes on the history of life on earth.

However it is our presence in that stretch of natural history, which brings to light the incredible extent of what we humans have managed to attain, from such humble beginnings as a species without any special physical endowments such as armor, claws, powerful teeth and the like possessed by other creatures.

We stood upright and used our wits to walk to the present, becoming on the way, a true force of nature, a force capable of doing in a very short time, things that only geological forces could accomplish over the span of millions of years.

The Holocene epoch is not just a geological time with an interesting story for scientists studying the dynamics and physical history of the earth, but it is to us, also a critical comparison chart of sorts upon which we can track and measure the magnitude of our capacity to change the world and for us living at present, a source of reliable evidence that can help us to come to grips with the reality that, that same capacity has also placed us along side with most other life on earth on a course of mass extinction.

I would propose that the focus here is not on what went wrong; rather I wish to focus on the portrait of humanity that emerges from our collective activity over the 11,700 years that comprise the Holocene epoch.

The reason is, that I hope to persuade you that the image that surfaces is not the image of a creature whose original design was to destroy the world, rather, what emerges is an image of humanity that is framed by the Holocene epoch to reveal an image of what is best described as our adolescence as a species.

The Holocene Landscape that we traversed across millennia until the present and the tracks of our presence in it, show us a landscape that in the whole, could be compared to how the average adolescent human treats his/her room at home, it begins beautiful and pristine and progressively gets more and more disorganized, things break, upkeep duties are ignored, discarded materials pile up, the air gets fowled up by various odors and before long, it is hard to call it a room because the image of a trashcan becomes irresistibly appropriate instead.

Perhaps more relevant still, is the adolescent attitude by humanity of knowing everything and ignoring parental advice (Nature) at all cost in favor of keeping up with what friends are doing and following the newest trend without any interest in detailed examination of effects and consequences.

While my comparison may look on the surface to be naïve and even ridiculous as a description of human presence throughout the Holocene epoch, we may see a lot more relevance if we take the time to scale it up from one person to a family group, to a neighborhood, to a town, to a state, to a nation, to a whole world of nations and look at their individual and collective histories and then look closely at the world only to see that the whole planet has indeed become everyone's trashcan.

I have to pause here for a moment to qualify the spirit behind this chapter that I call the Holocene Landscape.

The Holocene epoch is a remarkable period in the history of both the world and of humanity. It is a time in which the power of Nature began to be undermined by the power of human creativity, itself a powerful by-product of abstract thought and of our ability to think about thinking. That was a cognitive improvement we had acquired early in our development as a species, a development that allowed our species to set its own evolutionary course, unlike any other creature that had ever lived on earth before or since.

While our fundamental human-made survival strategy had been developing for a couple of million years or more before the Holocene epoch, it is worth noting that our activity although more sophisticated than that of all other creatures because of its creative ability and attributes, it nevertheless remains to this day firmly rooted and attached to very primitive impulses that are shared by all other living creatures.

The only thing that is unnatural about us is our interpretation of the world and our activity, outside of that our physical and fundamental conscious wiring remains largely natural.

The big difference is, that we have "amplified" the basic survival impulses we share with all other plant and animal life, (think of them as components of a basic survival tool kit) to deliberately create with them, the cultural context that distinguishes humanity as the makers of a civilization such as we have at present and of the world we are inhabiting.

Take for instance an impulse like aggression, which we have amplified from a survival defense mechanism of self-preservation into a full-blown culture of war characterized by astonishing acts of violence. A culture of war around which human civilization shapes its ambitions, its development, its social, political, religious, industrial and economic direction.

As this book is about a migration of the human mind towards a next best operative level that is favorable to human survival, the Holocene landscape that I'm referring to is not specific to the geological landscape and its history, rather is about the human mindscape as it unfolded throughout the Holocene epoch.

I do so, in order to create a reference that can help me to illustrate very briefly some of the highlights that account for the peculiar way that our presence and activity developed over the millennia to the present day.

That way, my narrative can have a kind of backdrop upon which the contrast between our activity in the Holocene and our activity in the Anthropocene will clarify the fundamental reasons for our new migration and the survival advantages that may come with it.

Migration in that context may be described as a departure from a perceived normality of mind, the way the world is perceived and the way we respond to that understanding of the world. Migrating from there to another level of perceived normality of mind, where a fresh new understanding modifies our responses to better suit our survival advantages, would place us in what is essentially a new world, the human-made world of the Anthropocene.

While it is difficult in fact impossible to find an example of mind-migration from one world to another since this is the first time that idea has come up, examples of mind-migration from one normal to another are abundant and the effect of the survival advantages that came from them did in fact, changed the course of human history.

Consider how the normality of hunting and gathering of food by our predecessors at the beginning of the Holocene migrated to a new normal that changed the course of human history. It all started from a very simple connection made (probably by women) between wild plants growing in the areas around the caves or camps, where discarded foodstuff containing seeds where involuntarily planted, followed by the seed's subsequent germination, growth and eventual harvest.

It follows that making the connection from that, to the idea of deliberately planting them was not long in coming nor was the birth of agriculture and farming. That cultural adaptation ended the hunting gathering tradition and placed humanity on the path to civilization (meaning, life in the city.)

There we have, one clear instance of migration of the human mind from one "normal" way of life to another, one could say that the sign over that transitional portal read "Welcome to the Holocene epoch."

It is from there on, where those basic survival impulses that I mentioned before, began to swell up in order to compensate for the demands of the Holocene epoch in which this new "normal" way of life apart from nature began to unfold.

It follows that with the advent of agriculture and later on the development of the first cities, the direction of humanity was "civilization" and all that it stands for now.

The development of the city and city life became the principal driver for the amplification of every primitive behavioral impulse as the demands of population growth, economic growth, city management, defense and of course the blossoming and ever more complex civilization's primary support systems meaning technology, government, science, industry, religion and media.

It is quite likely that life in the city was the principal agency behind the cultural departure, which progressively created the ever-growing demarcation of difference and of separateness between humanity and the world outside of the city.

It was the nurturing of civilization that seem to have influenced the nature of the human project as an independent initiative, where, Nature itself was to be no more than the willing provider of the required resources needed to accomplish the design and exigencies of the city.

In a way, the project to create our own human nature found within the city limits, the perfect incubator and it was from the city that we began to change the world. Sadly and quite innocently we began to change the world to feed the city, some 5,000 years before we obtained the detailed understanding of Nature, and of life itself that modern science has been revealing to us while at a time when the beauty and fragility of our world continues to be critically compromised by the human project and the upkeep of the city, that is, civilization.

The Holocene saw the rise of the first five independent civilizations in the history of the world, as they occurred in Iraq, Egypt, India, China, Central and South America. While each civilization developed a unique view of life, all of them did so utilizing the same basic cultural tool kit, that is, the same cognitive capacity and survival response impulses that our predecessors brought with them, when our species first migrated out of Africa.

The ancient Sumerian city of Uruk in Southern present day Iraq is thought to have been the first city, appearing some 5,000 years ago and becoming the cradle of civilization, it was there that the blue print for government, science, industry, religion and media was first drawn.

It is there, where we find a staggering number of first ever inventions that were motivated by the development and upkeep of the city, the first temple or ziggurat, the first king, the first law, the first great work of literature, the first writing, the first astronomy, the first time that time and space was divided in multiples of sixty, the first schools, the first map of the world, the first wheels, the first streets, the first markets, the first industries, the first war and sadly the first evidence that civilization and its demands on the environment also destroys the land. Uruk is the first example of the consequences of life in the city and its voracious appetite for goods and services.

It is from this incredible first blueprint of humanity's first effort at collective living in a city, where the star ups for the exponential growth that came from all of those firsts invented in Uruk, got on their way through time to the complexity that they harbor today in modern civilization.

That is therefore the template or pattern that gave the idea of living together in an organized large-scale urban society. It is that fundamental model, with all of the subsequent adaptations, changes and cultural variations, which constitutes the mindscape of human civilization in the Holocene epoch.

It is at this point in my narrative, where I will invite the reader to realize that the fundamental ideas behind civilization remain essentially the same to the present and that even if the cultural focus of each of the subsequent civilizations is notably different, they all share "Violence" as a common denominator.

The invention of war and the careful nurturing of a culture of war is still the main driver of all human enterprise placing the biggest demand on the city for its maintenance and upkeep.

Of course, what I mean by the city is the collective body of people, their individual place in the social structure, their specialty and the unique character of their enterprise, all of which contributes to the body and the spirit of life in the city and its larger attribute as civilization.

Here however, is where the mindscape gets more complex because the model of the first city has grown and evolved to become whole nations, same ideas, but at a vast scale. Civilization then has also evolved to encompass many nations, hundreds of them, and the city itself is now a global society with seven billion citizens competing for the same diminishing resources in order to keep the city alive.

In a way, human civilization has come this far in 5,000 years just to be in the same predicament as when the city of Uruk found itself demanding more from the environment than the environment could give and devastated the land; beginning thereby the slow disintegration of the city and its people. Uruk today is a memory sustained by a desolate and inhospitable landscape, a memory that we should have kept closely at hand as we made social, cultural and environmental choices.

The mindscape that we are contemplating as the end of the Holocene, is one of an unstoppable arrogant and voracious civilization, that is so invested, in the upkeep of an unsustainable way of life, that is lulled to denial by the pressures stemming from having no real answers, or ignoring answers that challenge the hegemony of the misguided innocence, of past and current makers of civilization.

The view of the Holocene-human-mindscape is made more honest and true by the fact that at this point in the history of life on earth, none of the pillars of civilization, meaning, government, the sciences, religion, industry and the media, has substantially delivered on any of their promises. Their combined effort has delivered the entire human species and the rest of the natural world onto a sacrificial altar, where life on earth, will be offered to the sixth mass extinction event unless we admit that if nothing is done about it, that is the fate of the city and of the world upon which civilization stands.

Like it or not we are Anthropocene creatures now and it is because of early scouts like me, that the narrative of the human project can look forward to a new beginning; not a beginning from scratch for our species, but, a beginning from now on. The closing of the Holocene epoch, has showed us with inescapable proof in the state of our world, the extent and consequences of the incompleteness of our survival strategy.

The opening of our journey through the Anthropocene and its inherit challenges; however, will set us on a transitional course to evolve culturally so as to fill in the missing pieces and to reorganize the world that our predecessors so innocently nearly destroyed.

"Cognitive Bubble"

Chapter III
Humanity's report card

Looking at our Holocene humanity from the Anthropocene perspective, is a very helpful way to see us truly from the world we created for ourselves and knowing from the observable results that what got us here, is in fact the result of a lot of effort tailored quite unfortunately, by an incomplete cultural context.

I'm talking about a human cultural practice that is incomplete, mainly because the only concerns we had throughout the Holocene epoch, where those of our own survival and those associated with the quest to conquer each other and the world.

Our Holocene cultural context always placed us outside of Nature and placed Nature at our disposition, with no concerns for plant, animal life or environment other than those that would provide direct benefit to us without a benefit return to Nature.

All of that worked rather well until now, however, Nature is giving but there is such a thing as a tipping point and we have arrived at it.

What I wish to share in this chapter, titled humanity's report card, is a kind of synthesis that underscores the state of our cultural context entering the Anthropocene. As I see no use for grading our adolescence as a species, or to bring to bear, our shortcomings as a species without redemption.

Therefore the report card simply states that at this time in history, we are exactly the result of the cultural context that we have been cultivating, since our distant ancestors first stood up some six million years ago and took a good look at the African savannah and somehow, decided that they could walk and think about their next move at the same time.

Discovering how to survive in the world for us, being as different as we are from all other animals was not easy, specially since at the time, there was no one able to tell the difference. Our ancestral lineage, was discovering an eat and be eaten world and every time we could up our survival stakes we did; that was good then and I'm sure it will also come in handy in the up and coming future.

We became good at spotting opportunity and before long we became good observers of the world; mimicking nature to prop up our survival strategy.

Take for instance the fact that life on the savannah includes periodic flash fires that strike unannounced and whose effect is to literally barbeque anything that can't get out of the way in time.

Enter our ancestor, possibly Homo erectus, who at the time had become adept at spotting freshly abandoned kills by other top predators and had learned to take advantage of the spoils. Now, move that skill forward and find our ancestor rushing in after the flash fire to find freshly killed and cooked meals way before the hyenas or other predators dared entering the scorched savannah.

Fast-forward the connection between fire and the benefit of soft cooked meat to find that before long, may be a few hundred years or even thousands of years, someone found the way to mimic the fire producing lighting with the strike of a fire flint while making a hand axe or rubbing two sticks together to mimic the burning branches from the flash fire. Well-done Homo erectus!

We did not invent fire we learned to mimic and control natural fire and brought it to the hearth to cook our food.

It is no small feat that from such a humble feat as using controlled fire, that we managed in 2012 to send with the use of fire a space craft that has left the solar system and is at present traveling in inter galactic space.

We have peered into the most intimate sanctum of life and learned that our DNA is intrinsically connected to all other creatures that live or that have ever lived and learned the inescapable conclusion, that we all share a common ancestor at the beginning of the miracle of life on earth.

At the same time we have found that planets that may host life forms like ours are not the most numerous in our galaxy in fact we still do not have one viable candidate in our sights.

We are without a doubt the first earth bound species that has ever looked at the past in such detail as to ascertain the conditions that where present at an infinitesimal moment after the big bang and the beginning of the universe that we are a part of.

We are also a species whose cultural context has not as yet or at least until now; found a way to measure ideas in the same way that we have learned to measure the visible universe or the distance of an electron from the nucleolus of a particular atom.

Not having that cultural instrument has placed us in an ongoing debate of wits about what is and what is not. It is a confusion of ideas where their relevance of time is not considered in the evaluation of their meaning and how their meaning has evolved over time.

Humanity as seen from the Anthropocene has to learn, that all histories and I mean each and every one of our contributing ideas over a span of millions of years is the material which make up the cultural context of humanity.

All of it is good because it is a part of the overall effect of the evolution of a species that thinks about thinking and that has done so for thousands of years.

Humanity does not have a right idea that is above all others; humanity has a menu of ideas that have to be organized into a composite where all ideas are contributing agents of an emerging reality that validates their origin and the order of ascendency that brought them to this critical point, where they all become, the foundations of the new vision for a species in transition to either extinction or to the next level on their evolutionary path.

We are a species that has managed for instance, to take greed to the point where we actually created room for a non-human corporate entity, which we endowed with the quality of a living being with all of the privileges of a person, who with our help has evolved to unilaterally overruled life itself, in exchange for a bottom line and a market-share that benefits no one but itself.

That is a corporate entity that has nothing to offer to its unsuspecting owners, other than a steady decline of the very environment upon which their own lives depend. The Anthropocene has a banner on its entry portal that reads; "regardless of what your plans for the future are, they cannot happen without air and water."

Corporations are nothing more than a realized figment of our imagination they are entities that cannot find beauty in a meadow unless there is oil beneath the surface. They are the masters of the world and humanity, nothing more than the patsy they use to achieve the goals that human greed programed into such corporations to achieve. They are a textbook example of short-term win long-term disaster.

Let me illustrate that point with something like it, occurring in the natural world but not quite as sinister.

There is a parasitoid called Dicrocoelium dentriticum who is what is known as a parasitic fluke. This interesting character uses the "ant" Formica fusca as an intermediary host, which somehow it manipulates into taking control of the ant's actions making it leave the colony and to climb atop a grass blade where it clings until a grazing animal comes along and eats the grass and the ant thereby reaching its goal to find the definitive host for its own life cycle.

The new corporate entity in the digital age may act like that parasite on the minds of sensible people who's greed allows the parasite to take control of their actions to become unwilling carries of a disaster whose definitive host is a world devoid of life as we know it.

The Anthropocene is not just a geological designation for the convenience of the stratigraphic society, it is in fact the most serious warning and the most recent challenge that our species has yet to face. It is our do or die as the stuff that gives the Anthropocene its character is a collection of the most toxic and foul after effects, of our age of plenty and inexhaustible resources, as tamed by science into the deadliest threat to life on earth.

We have also nurtured a scientific arrogance that suggests that in a few more decades of genetic engineering we should be able to overturn the work of billions of years of development by Nature or what surely is earth's signature feature in the evolution of life.

That is an innocent arrogance that was already at work 500 years ago, when Francis Bacon suggested that science and technology would conquer Nature so that humanity may become the master of the world and a law onto himself. Been there done that and now what?

Life is the most researched and at the same time the least understood of subjects because of our separateness from nature, we are deeply immersed in our own human nature trying to make sense of something to which we are not connected.

We do not even think of ourselves as a single species and we are. How could we even take the next step and be a part of nature when our own nature demands that we destroy the world in order to do what?

So far, it is mainly to meet the market expectations for a global corporate entity to which life is not a concern at all, while short-term profits are the primary concern of a very ill informed institutional imperative about the fundamental requisites of life on earth.

Ah, we are all in this and none of us is guilty, for innocence is the hallmark of adolescence. We did not know better and no one preplanned any of this.

Consider the fact that no form of government ever began as a tyranny by whatever name; rather, they came into existence as genuine efforts to deal with human conditions separated by wide gaps of class and inequality in the distribution of resources, the appropriation of mutual respect and the preservation of the ever-desired urge for freedom with a measure of happiness.

After 5,000 thousand years of recorded history no form of government has, nor can deliver a just and contented society, instead, we have learned to mask tyranny in a variety of gazes, not because we wish to do so but rather, because our cultural context cannot produce something it never had, something that we are just about to discover as we will see later on.

Similarly, we have religion operating within the same cultural context and currently at a loss for direction not because the fundamental ideals are not useful, but mostly because of the same cultural fatigue that plagues all of the organizing forces of human civilization and the burden of the great contradictions between what is professed and what actually gets done.

The arts are perhaps the greatest barometer measuring the cultural context of civilization during the Holocene epoch. From its earliest ambitions to portray the world we interpret within our minds to the last efforts of its modernity; nothing can rival art's ability to show us who we are and to confront us with what we have become.

Like all of the other principal institutions of civilization, the arts too have adapted to the

consumer frenzy and art itself has been made a
commodity, branding the artist and sadly
ensuring that the market determines the value,
meaning and direction of art.

But what do the arts show as a measure of our
cultural context?

Well, here is the golden kernel for this chapter
not only for the book but also, for this closing
chapter in the history of planet Earth; The
Holocene epoch.
The arts do dramatically mirror the state of
humanity more than art ever did before, because
of the dazzle of the technology that makes the
worldwide human spectacle, accessible
everywhere as if the event was occurring just
down the street.

The works themselves do reflect the fatigue of a
cultural context, which cannot offer anything new
as shown by the almost desperate efforts by a
new generation of artists, to try out what else can
be passed out as art.

Nowhere else is the alienation between
civilization and the world more evident or
presented with such exquisite clarity than in the
art of the last 50 years. The arts have done well in
exploring the depths of civilized life and have
exposed the far reaches of our capacity for
beauty, for shock and for horror as well as our

penchant for nothing, for sublimity, for goodness, for peace, for justice, for freedom, for expression and these days for a cleaner and more hospitable world.

The arts have another thing to tell us about what we have become as a species, we have become a collective of individuals. As ridiculous as that sounds, the culture and the environmental pressures of life in the city have ushered us into the cult of the self.

That is a cult that the arts show, as an internalized reflection of human society by the artist as his/her art is so deeply personal that the works are like black holes from which not even meaning escapes, save for those gestures that recall some relationship between the work and our personal experience whose meaning is not in the work but safely tucked away in our own mind. It is a cult of the; me first, me second, me third with no leftovers-sorry.

Art is nonetheless an outspoken voice for humanity and for all of its glory and shortcomings art is eloquently telling us that we have retreated into the self because collectively we cannot agree on anything. That is our generation's most significant signpost at the end of the Holocene, where humanity's greatest collective triumph was to "agree to disagree."

Happily that is also a telltale sign of our cultural incompleteness, as we have not as yet implemented a cultural instrument that allows us to go beyond agreeing to disagree.

There is virtually, not an issue in whatever field of inquiry that is not marred by disagreement and consequently stalled or doomed to remain unproductive even if it means the difference between success and failure.

That cultural deficiency has all but corralled humanity into an age of awareness where critical problems cannot go beyond awareness because there is not sufficient agreement to formulate even weak plans of action.

I have listened to some of the most enlightened scientists and intellectuals, present their studies, their findings and observations to eager audiences who want to know and act, only to conclude their presentations with a now familiar phrase at the end of their talks; " friends, we have a problem and it is time that we do something about it; thank you very much."

That is it?

What is now hotly debated as climate change and global warming are concerns that where first voiced 150 years ago in relation to the industrial release of carbon dioxide into the atmosphere.

We have been "aware" of that and many other perils but we are also unable to do something about them, because we are also at the cultural edge of our cognitive capacity to go beyond agreeing to disagree.

That cultural instrument is already here, as we will discover in later chapters and it is because of that cultural instrument and a few others that I do not need to presume to give humanity a failing mark in our Holocene report card.

We have done everything that brought us this far and all of it is ours, we are an adolescent species whose incomplete cultural context could not have done much different than that.

Well-done Homo sapiens; we made it to the Anthropocene epoch. Fasten your seat belt because it is going to be one hell of a ride.

"Follow Life"

Chapter IV
Welcome to the Anthropocene epoch

Well, without any further adieu from the Holocene… Welcome to the Anthropocene epoch!

Sometimes things happen in life that we could not possibly just make up by ourselves and yet there they are.

I titled this book The Next Great Migration for a good reason and that is that by the time that Eugene Stoermer originally coined a term, which later on Paul Crutzen independently reinvented and called the Anthropocene epoch, borrowing from the Greek anthropo meaning "human" and scene meaning "new" which is widely presented as the Age of Man (a bit sexist) or just the epoch of the human made world.

As I was saying, by the time a name was given to the obvious transformation of planet Earth going on as the result of human intervention, I was already scouting that new world without a name for it, but, a world with ever more abundant data indicating that we had indeed crossed the bridge between the Holocene epoch and this now named Anthropocene epoch.

In 1981, I placed in Cape Coral, Florida, a large sculpture called the "Rubicond" (page 48) which is a word coined from the name of the Rubicon River and in reference to the legendary crossing of the river by Julius Caesar and the momentous circumstances attending the crossing of the river into Italy proper, with a standing army in January 49 BC, a move that was deemed as treason but one that Julius calculated as the next best move of his campaign but also one that forebode a point of no return, as he proclaimed "the die is now cast"

While the Rubicond did not proclaim the Anthropocene epoch it did proclaimed the now fact, that civilization had crossed the point of no return. The Rubicond was not a stratigraphic marker but it is a cultural evolutionary marker as the creature it presents is a transgenic creature of our own making a creature made from snippets of various plant and animal DNA sequences.

The work's message is the cultural equivalent of the Anthropocene message of change so radical as to become the basis for the definition of a new world. The Rubicond's message heralds the end of Nature's imperative over the design of life and the beginning of the design of life according to human specifications.

Rubicond sculpture 1981

In short, we had taken charge of life for the
benefit of our own ambitions within the
framework of civilization with no real knowledge
of the intimate process of life or its carefully
tailored interconnectivity to all life in the past,
present or future.
We crossed the point of no return with the same
kind of short-term innocence as Julius Caesar,

not knowing that soon after he will be assassinated and that the Roman Empire itself will come to an end in 475 AD.

The Rubicond shows us a creature whose being is thrust upon a landscape to which it has no past kinship, no real place in the present or a true interconnected role to play in the future of life. The Rubicond is just a freak, to account for human achievement in an increasingly monetized and patent ridden ownership of life's hereditary history, a history whose sovereignty stayed on the far shore of the Holocene.

Here in the Anthropocene, Genetic engineering will be a critical instrument for the preservation of life but not for the preservation of human arrogance and greed as they are at present, as those qualities of human culture must too evolve to suit life.

This is a world we made up with our creative capacity and by the same token it is a world that only our creative capacity can and should deliver us from the effects that our activity as an adolescent and innocent species has exposed us all, it was our short-term vision, our selfish abandon to our reason and the incomplete cultural context which conquered the world and led us to an empty victory.

Human civilization has not failed yet, civilization has only to evolve to remain, the great human project that we began 5,000 years ago.

To be sure, the Anthropocene landscape is horrendous and the task to put it back in order will seem unbearable at times but it can be done. We not only owe it to ourselves, to our children but to life itself and the fact that we have come a long way and should still go a long way ahead.

Welcome to the Anthropocene is an invitation to take a first step into the reality of our time, so that the magnitude of a global event such as the Anthropocene epoch, may give us reference of the scale and breath of that reality, of its implications, of the very threat of extinction that we face.

Therefore just admitting that however severe or misguided our appraisal of the world is at the moment, we are in it nonetheless and admitting to it is a great first step.

A first step like that is the true star-up of humanity's conscious migration into this new Anthropocene world, but greater still, is the fact that what is set in motion is no less than the cultural evolution that will provide the direction, the means and the tools to navigate through it.

There is much confusion and misinformation floating out there, respecting whether or not the Anthropocene is or is not a proper Geological epoch, or that its adoption as a proper geological epoch division is too riddled with disagreement, as it is typically the case with new science and the two sided arguments, by many scientists who challenge the propriety of suggested beginning dates and the validity of primary ecological markers that have been presented and so on.

While these important discussions are occurring however, there is a very strong consensus that the Anthropocene is the best description of the world today, that we are in the midst of its occurrence and that, when the Stratigraphic commission of the Geological Society of London finally grants the Anthropocene a formal adoption into the geological time scale, most of the world would have already heard of it by then and would have adopted the Anthropocene epoch into the culture.

That does not mean that the effects associated with the name or with the continued impact of human activity upon the entire world biosphere are changed in any way by the acceptance of a name for something that we already know is out there.

The Eskimos have been reporting weather abnormalities and changes in the polar environment for decades, Farmers around the world have also reported sustained environmental changes in crop production and seasonal irregularity, the South American Andean communities have pointed to dramatic snowcap reduction and of migration by plant and animals life to higher altitudes from their long held historic habitats.

There is much evidence that the ice polar caps are melting at a prodigious rate, that ancient glaciers are also disappearing whilst low land coastal areas around the world are flooding beyond recent all time high historical levels.

As I said before, the new world by whatever name is already here and we are in it. The question is how soon and how smart are we going to be in accepting that fact.

The current division between climate change advocacy and the corresponding opposition for instance, is only a transparent convenience of the institutional imperative, in response to perceived notions of profit loss, diminishing power and fear of retribution for wrong doing, in the face of non existing instruments that can mediate their transition to more productive grounds where they may operate at a fraction of their current environmental foot prints.

On one hand, the Anthropocene is not permissive of human denial when it comes to life itself, some people may say all they want about denial of conditions and their cause but, that does not change or improve the conditions or the cause. When a natural system is disrupted the disruption does not wait for our approval or for the culprits to go to trial, as they say, when the volcano erupts it does at its own discretion without the need for our approval.

On the other hand, The Anthropocene epoch is mostly our handy work and as such, we have the ability to change it, which is perhaps the most important card we have to play in the survival game in years to come.

Once acceptance is reached, that we humanity are indeed the masters of our fate, a fact that is made ever more evident, by the very existence of a whole world of our own making emerging as proof of the collective power of our species to change the world. What I'm saying is that the world that we almost destroyed in innocence is also a world, which we can collectively restore, in full knowledge of its exquisite and delicate nature and in the light that life itself is the most precious commodity.

The emerging question therefore is not whether we can do it, but rather, are we willing to do it?

I think we do indeed, because the most fundamental impulse of all living creatures is to live, a fact that is demonstrated by our species in the almost inconceivable amount of resources, money, time and effort humanity spends in the pursuit of health, beauty and well being.

The rigors of the Anthropocene will bring life in general into sharp focus by the increased occurrence of its absence and the growing despair that scarcity brings into the lives of hungry people competing for the last pockets of resources that the world cannot replenish anymore.

You may have heard of the cataclysmic reduction in the ocean's fish stock and very likely also heard someone pronounce the alarm as sounded by oceanic scientists as rubbish. A typical response is that there is more fish left than the fish numbers scientists suggest in their proposed stock approximate counts.
While the numbers may be not be accurate to the last fish, our consumption and waste of the ocean fauna is not, nor is our disregard to the fact that at the same time, our other activities have turned the ocean into a trash-can with real rubbish and in such quantities that their effect has already changed significantly the ocean's ability to nourish the fauna or the flora that lies at the base of all ocean life.

That is only the ocean portion of our Anthropocene landscape, the land does not fare any better nor does the atmosphere nor does the rigors of the similar style mass exploitation of the human resource going on, all, in the name of a number of misguided notions of possession wealth and power at all cost that are fueled and powered by primitive impulses that we inherited from our primordial ancestors. Impulses like territorial possession of a food resource in a small patch of the forest still practiced by the chimpanzee and other primates, an impulse, which we amplified to the territorial possession of the whole world.

I mentioned the amplification of the impulse of possession to be able to use that fact as the canvas upon which to paint a picture of the Anthropocene which I believe human eyes have never seen the likes of it because it is an image of ourselves which could have never been imagined during the Holocene epoch.

Allow me to explain, When we entered the Holocene epoch, we humans were a number of small bands of people, engaged in the process of expanding our presence and our interpretation of the world into what today we know as "human nature," that is, the development of a unique view of the world through our own eyes, or you may think of it as, one specie's interpretation of life independent from the way millions of other animal and plant species interpret the push and pull of environmental conditions along with the organic exchange of nutrients that constitute the collective life force, which sustains the process we call, life on earth.

Let us keep in mind that the Anthropocene epoch and all of its challenges are for the most part, the results coming from that independent interpretation of life, which we know as human nature, as expressed by human culture and its activity.

It follows that during the Holocene it was we against nature in every respect, as we relentlessly shaped nature to suit the design of our own nature. Later on with the advent of the city we accelerated that process and added huge and inventive escalations to our creative power to change the world.

As it stands the Anthropocene has two clear prospects for humanity and they are: One. Stay on the present course, use the remaining of the natural resources and go extinct as the environment collapses like a house of cards and the human order unleashes anarchy such as the world has never seen; as the city lights go out. Two. We begin to migrate consciously and embrace a cultural evolutionary path towards a better survival strategy that has life at the core of its thesis.

As this book is about the migration alternative, I will now paint in words that image of our species, which I said, could have never been seen before or more precisely has never existed in the context of human observation before.

It really is a case in which just as the grin of victory over nature and the world was at its brightest for the human species, as the reality of the empty victory began to set in and dissolve the grin into a grimace. Yes we did it, but at what cost? Yes we have technology good enough to send space probes to intergalactic space but we cannot stop ourselves from destroying the only world we have.

It is as if in the hour of our greatest achievement we are notified that the price attached to it, is the death of civilization and the ruin of all that we worked for.

In that context, the Anthropocene is a rallying call to life and an exhortation for the human species to take its rightful place in it and evolve to meet the defiance against life that our own adolescence as a species brought about.

In the Anthropocene, Life itself defines the terms of engagement and as living creatures our arrogance is not exempt from a process to which all life is not only intrinsically connected but that as a whole, none can exist in an environment that is toxic to the very essence and design of such connectivity.

The wealthiest person in the world cannot order a tuna fish sandwich that does not contain mercury, nor does he or she can survive without water or air without the specific properties that life like ours requires. Nor would the virtual computers, which run the world at present oblivious of the worth of life, can survive operative for long, without their human hosts and other life forms like us, as they are parasites totally dependent on the exploitation of the world until they are reprogramed from service to human greed to serve the interest of life on earth.

Here in the Anthropocene the Human/Nature relationship takes a considerable turn as life itself takes center stage, Human nature will come to grips with its incompleteness by the contrast created in the wake of the new cultural instruments that it was missing throughout the length of its adolescence.

Those cultural instruments are truly Anthropocene developments that will trigger the cultural evolution that will bring humanity, in concert with nature and allow for a reconciliation of sorts.

That reconciliation engenders the basis for the partnership between Nature and Human nature, which will form the basis of the joint recovery of life on earth. That alternative was never contemplated before, because human arrogance forbade equality between our kind and the rest of life on earth.

It is now that we know that although a single cell organism cannot hold a dialog about market prices or mathematical equations, a collectivity of 10 trillion of them are what makes you, and it is their collective effort in partnership with 200 trillion separate bacterial cells what powers your very existence whatever you do.

Keep in mind that while their physical integrity is in accord with the integrity of life on Earth, you get to live, when it is not you die; whoever you are.

Therein is a powerful message for our Anthropocene perspective and that is, that if 10 trillion cells can get together to make someone like you function what could stop 7 billion of us from beginning to restore our world if we decide to do so.

We are already in partnership with nature at the most fundamental and personal level, extending that to the rest of the world as a global partnership is the most natural thing we will ever do.

The Anthropocene is not a nice place at present but it is the only place we have, it will get worst for a while but not so bad that if we are working together we cannot endure. It will take hundreds of years before a generation is born to praise our labors but what a lovely incentive it is to know that it can happen.

Particularly in the face of an inevitable 6th mass extinction event that has already began and that we without losing face, can short-circuit at the drop of a hat.

"CEGE"

Chapter V
CEGE the great Anthropocene menace

We humans have a long, very long tradition of imaginative pursuits in the creation of monsters; it is hard to find a culture however primitive or civilized at any time in human history that does not have some extraordinary creature tormenting and casting fear over the people.

These legendary and fictional characters have been historically added to the horror of evil and all of its literary stars. However, the root of "monstrum" is "monere" which oddly enough means, warm as well as to instruct; the modern English word "Demonstrate" is therefore formed from those basis.

Curiously the theologian Saint Augustine saw the monster as a sign of instruction, which is why I chose to speak of monsters at the beginning of this chapter. It follows that Saint Augustine did not see the monster as necessarily evil, but as a kind of freak resulting from some error in the "natural design of the world."

Well, the monster that I'm going to introduce you to, is not a freak error in the natural design of the world, but it is a freak error of the "human-nature" design, of the world that we created for ourselves and is a potent sign of instruction for humanity in the years to come.

While I have to take credit for identifying and naming the monster, I did so without much pleasure as it is as hideous as it is destructive and the worst part of it is that sadly it is not a figment of my imagination. This puppy has been in plain sight for decades and if no one had seen it before is just because no one was looking.

I named it with the acronym CEGE that stands for "Compounded Environmental Global Effect," which is the sum total of all of the social, environmental and conservation issues rolled into one.

Think of the Greek myth of the Chimera, a fire breathing three-headed monster with one head of lion, one of a snake, and another of a goat, lion claws in front and goat legs behind, and a long snake tail.

Now try to picture CEGE as a real human-made monster with the body of a fish and a lashing tongue with a hundred or more tentacles, each capable of specific environmental harm. I do not really know how many there really are because every time I look at it carefully I see more tentacles on it.

While the CEGE effect really exists and is active all over the world, the form that I have attributed to it is imagined and I did so to make its "sign of instruction" visible as Saint Augustine suggests and its status as a monster more familiar culturally.

I gave it the body of a fish because CEGE is in a way the current apotheosis or the evolutionary triumph of a fish that came onto land over 300 million years ago and evolved into the first creature capable of changing the course of Natural life on earth.

The lashing tongue and its many tentacles are the nauseating effects of civilization coming from the activity to sustain a culture whose independence from the world, blinded humanity from cause and consequence of its actions, so long as the city could grow and the natural resources would hold for consumption, whatever the cost.

CEGE has remained invisible in whole, only because we chose to see one or two tentacles at a time and entertain ourselves in the ever-present game of admission and denial, an unfortunate game that effectively redirects public attention on the issues to the circus of political arguments, corporate finger pointing, religious environmental activism and social numbness on the crisis to name a few.

Climate change and global warming are two favorites at the moment, which aside from their critical nature, they are a source of the most revealing instances of human innocence. Take for instance the statement by a 2016 candidate to the presidency of the United States on climate change; "The climate is changing but we don't know who's to blame."

Could you imagine anyone saying; "The house is burning, the children are still inside but we would not call the fire department until we know who or what started the fire."

There is hilarity in what we say, but the fun stops at the reality of the crisis. Holocene human-culture cannot see beyond its limitations simply because it has not learned to admit that there are cultural limitations, that all of this chaos is the result of an active energetic but incomplete human cultural context.

Those limitations become not only visible but also irrefutable as the Anthropocene epoch comes trumpeting in the evidence of where those limitations lie.

CEGE is not only an eye opener but also the biggest surprise for humanity that our handy work has to offer. CEGE reveals with no holding back the severity of our terms of engagement with the Anthropocene epoch and the vastness of our inability to deal with it in the absence of real instruments to do so.

I think this is a good place to unpack CEGE a bit more so that we all begin to discover the monster for what it really is and I will try to do so in two different ways.

The first is a bit technical but mandatory description of Compounded Environmental Global Effect or CEGE, which is loosely defined; as the result from the combination of two or more disruptive toxic or harmful agents, whose individual action has a particular measurable effect upon a given environment, but, whose effect in association with other equally disruptive agents, precipitates a systemic avalanche that progressively overwhelms the capacity of the environment to maintain the biological equilibrium needed to sustain complex and interconnected ecosystems and thereby, instigating a planetary escalation that results in the global collapse of biological life as we know it here on Earth.

Described one other way, CEGE is the consequence that comes as the result of the combination of two or more different kinds of pollution that are harmful enough to the environment on their own, but that when mixed together create combined effects that like the domino-effect knock off one system after the other but in this case each domino is bigger than the one before and the last domino is life as we know it on Earth.

Allow me to unpack that definition a little bit more; CEGE is by far not your average villain, as an enemy CEGE's only objective is the eradication of life, all life. That is so because CEGE is made out of stuff that is toxic to life, all life. May be some form of life can again regain a footing but it would not be anything like life as we know it.

You may recall that there have been at least 5 previous mass extinction events in Earth's history and also that life returned and built upon the leftovers. We are a product of the last leftovers, however this time is not natural systemic agents like meteors, volcanoes or tectonic activity driving this next extinction event, rather, it is the toxic leftovers of our activity, an activity that never really had anything to do with life.
As the Native American old man said whilst looking at the destruction of his ancestral forest "people are the only animals who chop down and burn, the tree upon which they want to build their home." Sometimes the simplest observation can carry a deeply profound meaning.

CEGE is as I said a formidable enemy of life, but life in many ways and many levels is still a mystery to us and that is perhaps why we never saw this one coming. You see, we are used to think of the enemy as another human with comparable weaponry and a penchant for destruction, looting and an insatiable taste for violence, all in pursuit of a power victory and the spoils of war.

That is not the case with CEGE; this enemy is a multilevel insurgent that operates to infiltrate the biological chemistry of life from the smallest microscopic organisms to the largest and most complex creatures and everything in between. As I write this book, there is hardly a creature left that does not already have a generous endowment of plastic within their bodies even within the cell membrane.

Not only that but, CEGE also systematically disables the biological main frame for the extended food supplies of all of the contributors to the food chain from plankton to whales in the sea where ocean acidification is wreaking havoc, to the land where hot spots and pollution are devastating the micro fauna and flora; affecting bacterial integrity and the entire subsequent food chain to plant, insect and animal life.

Then, as if that was not enough, CEGE goes on to redefine the climatic conditions, the distribution of the glacial and polar water reserves, changes the atmospheric conditions and the chemistry of the air supplies and rains upon the land a toxic rain designed to destroy the arboreal oxygen supply and the oceanic oxygen supplies for all life.

Meanwhile, humanity works 24/7 to add to CEGE's power and strength with non-stop depletion of resources for the wanton consumption that is accelerating CEGE's rampant and wholesale destruction of life on planet Earth.

But wait a minute that is not all folks, CEGE has already infiltrated civilization's core, it has moved right into the city, right into the culture and all but hijacked human consciousness to do its betting. What!

That is right, you see, CEGE is an enemy to life but to itself CEGE is just an "effect" a result from our specific activity. Therefore the city is the biggest supplier of raw materials that contribute to the development and strength of its many tentacles, of course a consumer culture is the funding source for the creation of the materials themselves.

Now, the consciousness that feeds a consumer society in spite of humanity's true innocence, given the fact that if people really knew what they are doing, no amount of persuasion would induce rational people to destroy the only world they have.

It is the veneer of progress for short-term benefits, which drives civilization to make bad bets against its future, and it is in the spoils of these bets that CEGE would seem to have hijacked human consciousness to sustain the very pace that makes CEGE such formidable foe.

To my mind none of the bad bets would have been possible if human consciousness had been just a bit beyond from "awareness of one's existence" to "knowledge of one's existence within the concert of life.

That sounds weird at first but here is an inescapable comparison. Everything that exists in this universe is permissible by its own laws, but not everything that exists in the human mind is permissible. The reason is that the universe is a wholly unified entity and the human mind is not.

Just look at us living in a city with millions of strangers, divided by class, by race, by religion, by politics, by education, by life style and by a succession of petty, made up differences that keep us pinned against ourselves in the awareness zone while we miss the big picture, unconsciously working together for our own demise.

All or nearly all of the monsters that we have created before for our amusement live in our imagination and on books and DVD's. The harm they create other than fright is imaginary, CEGE on the other hand is really here, is palpable, it is constantly growing in strength and we feed it daily.

CEGE is as unique as the circumstances that created it, if I have given it the character of a monster, which it surely is, is also because I needed to make CEGE visible to the human conscious by giving CEGE a shape and the status of an single entity whose combined aim is the end of life as we know it.

CEGE's status as an enemy is a perfect fit for a civilization nurtured by war from its infancy, sustained by war, inspired by a culture of war and also threatened to complete annihilation by the instruments of war.

One of CEGE's most powerful tentacles, is nuclear waste and radioactive spills, not that the other ones are not deadly, it is that this one actually changes the time scale at which we can react to do something remedial about it once it is set lose.

Radioactive materials are processes that do not mix well with life as they are of an entirely different class and scale in their association with our development as living beings.

That is to say that they are perfectly natural processes, our sun for instance is what is called a main-sequence star and produces life giving energy but in its proper context and at 91.4 million miles way from us. You place the sun next door and what you get is Fukushima and all these other calamities waiting to happen.

At the same time, one may recalled that nuclear fission was developed for war and destruction. The latter applications are again short gain irresponsible investments in the "light" that our sun can provide civilization with energy for another 5 to 6 billion years at no charge.

We have found so many ways to kill each other and yet we still have not found a way to learn how to live with life.

As evil and devastating as CEGE really is, it is also a harbinger of untold opportunity for the future of civilization and for the continuation of life on earth. We the perennial warrior has finally found an enemy worthy of our zeal to do battle.

I do not wish to give you here a catalog of CEGE's tentacles, however if you dare to look them up just search for "list of environmental issues" and make sure you are sitting down when you do, because that is just the beginning.

Following is a partial list just to get your acquaintance with CEGE started...
Climate change — Global warming • Global dimming • Fossil fuels • Sea level rise •

Greenhouse gas • Ocean acidification • Shutdown of thermohaline circulation • Environmental impact of the coal industry • Urban Heat Islands • Flooding
Environmental degradation — Habitat destruction • Invasive species
Environmental health — Air quality • Asthma • Birth defect • Developmental disability • endocrine disruptors • Environmental impact of the coal industry •Environmental impact of nanotechnology • Electromagnetic fields • Electromagnetic radiation and health • Indoor air quality • Lead poisoning • Leukemia •Nanotoxicology •Nature deficit disorder •One Health • Sick Building Syndrome • Environmental impact of hydraulic fracturing
Environmental issues with energy — Environmental impact of the coal industry • Environmental impact of the energy industry • Environmental impact of hydraulic fracturing •
Environmental issues with war - Agent Orange • Depleted Uranium• Military Superfund site (Category only)•Scorched earth • War and environmental law • Unexploded ordnance
Overpopulation — Burial • Overpopulation in companion animals • Tragedy of the commons • Gender Imbalance in Developing Countries • Sub-replacement fertility levels in developed countries•
Genetic engineering — Genetic pollution • Genetically modified food controversies

Pollution — Nonpoint source pollution • Point source pollution •
Air pollution — Environmental impact of the coal industry • Environmental impact of hydraulic fracturing • Indoor air quality • Smog • Tropospheric ozone • Volatile organic compound Atmospheric particulate matter CFC • Biological effects of UV exposure
Light pollution • Visual pollution •
Noise pollution •
Soil pollution — Alkali soil •Brownfield • Residual Sodium Carbonate Index • Soil conservation • Soil erosion • Soil contamination • Soil salination • Superfund• Superfund sites
Space debris • Interplanetary contamination * Ozone depletion
Water pollution — Acid rain •Agricultural runoff •Algal bloom • Environmental impact of the coal industry • Environmental impact of hydraulic fracturing• Eutrophication • Fish kill •Groundwater contamination• Groundwater recharge • Marine debris • Marine pollution • Mercury in fish • Microplastics • Nutrient pollution • Ocean acidification • Ocean dumping • ocean pollution •Oil spills• Soda lake •Ship pollution • Thermal pollution • Urban runoff • Wastewater
Resource depletion — Exploitation of natural resources • Overdrafting (groundwater) •Overexploitation
Consumerism — Consumer capitalism • Planned obsolescence • Over-consumption

Fishing — Blast fishing • Bottom trawling • Cyanide fishing • Ghost nets • Illegal, unreported and unregulated fishing • Overfishing • Shark finning • Whaling

Logging — Clearcutting • Deforestation • Illegal logging

Mining — Acid mine drainage • Environmental impact of hydraulic fracturing • Mountaintop removal mining • Slurry impoundments

Water (depletion) — Anoxic waters • Aral Sea • California Water Wars • Dead Sea • Lake Chad • Water scarcity

Toxicants — Agent Orange • Asbestos • Beryllium • Bioaccumulation • Biomagnification • Chlorofluorocarbons (CFCs) • Cyanide • DDT • Endocrine disruptors • Explosives • Environmental impact of the coal industry • Herbicides • Hydrocarbons • Perchlorate • Pesticides • PBDE • Persistent organic pollutant • PBBs • PBDEs • Toxic heavy metals • PCB • Dioxin • Polycyclic aromatic hydrocarbons • Radioactive contamination • Volatile organic compounds

Waste — Electronic waste • Great Pacific Garbage Patch • Illegal dumping • Incineration • Litter • Waste disposal incidents • Marine debris • Medical waste • Landfill • Leachate • Toxic waste • Environmental impact of the coal industry • Exporting of hazardous waste.

Note:
The previous partial list of environmental issues
was sourced from Wikipedia the free
Encyclopedia – many thanks!

We have identified many of them for their unique
character but we have not even asked the
question about their interactivity, mainly because
CEGE that is the idea of seeing the face of the
environmental crisis landscape, as a
compounded global effect is something you are
reading here for the first time.

Science will do well to explore, untangle,
understand, explain and react to CEGE now that
art has conceived of its concealed existence.

CEGE is what you may call an Anthropocene
phenomenon, an inescapable feature of the
epoch we are in, an incentive for the human spirit
to rise above its adolescence and embrace its
adult responsibilities to life as a living being.

CEGE is an Anthropocene feature that no one
did or could have ever anticipated in the
Holocene, but CEGE is the human-made-spirit
driving the 6th mass extinction event.

The reality of CEGE, at least for starters, will
quench the small fires of denial about some of
the contributing issues and give bodies like the
UN's Intergovernmental Panel on Climate

Change (IPCC) a larger plate to show to the world's leadership and a real enemy that all of the people of the earth can find worthy of their collective effort to combat before it is too late.

The battle against CEGE is our first battle for life, is the first ever battle where we enlist all of life on Earth to active duty and all of our genius to create the weapons and the military tactics to combat the first real monster in the history of the Earth.

As with all storms, there is always a rainbow, CEGE will either destroy us of give us the way to unify our species and to unify our species with the world as that is the likely aftermath of this battle for life and the passport for life in our world to continue living.

"Art and Life Reconciled"

Chapter VI
Data-A – an Anthropocene aesthetic

Thank you for coming along with me this far, I know that one thing is to talk about what's going on and an entirely different thing is to do something about it.

Well this is where we begin to face the Anthropocene epoch with our best shot, our imagination and fortunately with the harvesting of ideas that I planted and cultivated over several decades and whose first blossoms and fruit are now, to my mind, indispensable new fare in the Anthropocene.

As we so crudely and briefly scampered over the Holocene epoch to get here, it is all too obvious that to engage that epoch in greater detail would have required a separate book. On one hand I'm confident that the existent body of written evidence is sufficient but on the other hand if you reference it, do it somewhat acrobatically as there is also a lot of misinformation out there.

The Anthropocene is truly a new and unexplored world and since this is a conscious migration, this new world is mostly about information, in fact a whole universe of information that can be expressed in ways that human inquiry never did.

Just as with the end of adolescence, adulthood comes with new responsibilities, so does the new world of the Anthropocene come with new characteristics to which we must also learn to respond to and address effectively as a species.

As you may already suspect the migration is very real, ready or not, as the Holocene bus is now parked in the lot of Earth's history with all of the other epochs that came before it and we are here with no way to go but forward.

While the Anthropocene may be a new world to us, we are from an older one and our cultural luggage has a lot of history and its own particular aesthetic.

Aesthetic is an idea that has been a bit blurry in our discourse perhaps because as with most other word-ideas that we have explored extensively, but that we have not really bothered to update or further unpack, their fundamental meaning.

Hopefully and out of necessity I may be able to take off a little of the murkiness to show you another layer that goes with the original idea but that together, the two fit rather well in the new world.

"Aesthetic" is about perception by the senses and about the interpretation by the mind of that which is perceived and further about the meaning that consciousness assigns to the way in which a perception is organized into the context of a given experience.

Aesthetic therefore relates to the kind of response that an experience elicits in terms of emotions that embrace notions of beauty or lack of beauty that are inherent on a given experience and directly related to the pattern of taste that results from it.

That is perhaps enough to suggest that our idea of the beautiful and conversely of the ugly also evolved parallel with our interpretation of the world over thousands of years, all of which gave rise to important aspects of our own unique human nature.

Still even our most inspired ideal of beauty or ugliness is still just our species unique idea and as we now know, the world that grew alongside our aesthetic, did not turned out to be so beautiful after all.

Again there is nothing terribly right or terribly wrong with our aesthetic, it is best to say at this point and at the beginning of this new world, that it is incomplete.

The most widely accepted late Holocene art, for instance, was a kind of glorification of the abstract conception that nothing itself can be beautiful, that meaninglessness was a quality of experience and that ugly and beautiful where after all just the two mirrors upon which we gazed our incompleteness as human beings. Further, that a very closed corridor between them, kept us from discovering life and the aesthetic of being free, from any restrains attached to a fixed egocentric perspective.

There are many real triumphs made on our six million year journey from hominids to here and as we contemplate the conscious migration that lies ahead. One triumph in particular is that over millennia we became particularly good at recording our cultural journey specially the founding civilization that saw the preservation of history as an important part of their culture.

This is critically important to us, not just for this chapter but also for the prospects of our new migration and that is, that history recorded in writing, in tales, in song, in ritual are great preservers of "information."

Aesthetic(s) therefore is principally about information and information is the key to understanding our individual and collective history as a species, our history as part of the development of life on Earth and on to the history of histories, the universe.

It follows then, that at the height of the Holocene epoch humanity had taken the idea of information to an all time high level of efficiency technologically, in fact the period was called the information age and subsequently the world was wired together into a single Internet network. Elsewhere science was putting together supercomputers to analyze information at phenomenal speeds and volumes. How about that!

While a lot if not most of the genius has been used for the usual priorities of defense and the goals of the institutional imperative of owning the world. The rest has given humanity very important benefits in many worthy fields of inquiry.

One in particular, at least for our immediate purpose is the field of astrophysics and cosmology. Let me explain, while there are thousands of things that we cannot agree upon for as many reasons or more, chances are that we agree on the fact that we are in a universe of sorts, whatever the cultural level of the observer. If you have eyes you have seen the stars, if you cannot see you have been told about them. The more you understand about the universe the closer you come to the inevitable conclusion that there is at least one universe and that we are in it, along with everything else.

That is where all of this has been about, because now we come to the kernel of this chapter.

Science tell us quite appropriately that the entire universe or universes as may be the case, are underscored by one common denominator and that is that the universe (S) is or are information or are made out of information; that being so, which it is, makes our world and us information too.

Information may be just one way of understanding the universe but it is a good way because the universe provides plenty of proof that the universe itself and everything in it has a story and that story is only available when you read the information that describes the story.

Our civilization has made the progress it has made because we have learned how to read the history of the universe to the extent that we have.

Here we come to a point where what can be called the Holocene mentality and the Anthropocene mentality requires some differentiation.

The Holocene mentality is by choice independent of nature, which is human made and made exclusively for human consumption, hence the idea of "Human nature." One can call that independent nature and all of its history, an "information stream" and that is fine, in fact that is exactly what it is.

The Anthropocene mentality however, should conserve its human nature but must also add on to it, because in acknowledging that the human information stream is incomplete as evidenced by the state of the world it created, more of the same would definitely not do.

Therefore a separate information stream would have to be invoked and added onto the human information stream, to form an information partnership in this case with Nature and thereby improve the context of the human information stream. Is that cuckoo or what?

Not at all, in fact that is the key or better yet, that is the ticket to our conscious migration into this new Anthropocene world. Please keep in mind, that it was ideas that got us here and therefore it would be ideas, fresh ideas, what will get us to the next stop.

Getting back to information itself, meaning, the universe as information, human nature as information and the state of our world as information, we can begin to see that there is an informational thread that kind of stiches all of them together. Now, if we take Nature as the thread that is the common denominator and allow nature to be the universal stream of information, then the nature we find on Earth is the same nature that we find in our version of it and both are part of the same nature that describes the universe itself as information. It is no coincidence that the word-idea Nature, describes the essence, the principle, the process, the body of the universe's own being.

What other information stream could we tap on to partner with than with the information stream to which we are but a small information thread whose obstinacy has placed its survival in peril but also at the threshold of a new and wonderful experience.

Now I would like to introduce you to Data-A; I coined the word to integrate the universal information stream with our human information stream as data, thereby forming one single stream of consciousness. Now since this is the first time in our history that we go out of our nature to learn from an older and more qualified teacher Nature itself, I added the suffix −A to highlight our new conscious excursion as plan A.

Which if you think about it, is exactly the case, I'm an Anthropocene scout of sorts and I have been here for decades but I do not have all of the answers nor pretend to know more than I do. This migration is in that respect akin to that of the Monarch butterfly, which takes several generations of Monarchs to reach their destination.

My life's work has been just to get us going on the right direction. The work and the direction will have to be improved, recalibrated and updated as we go, by people more qualified than I am. Thus Data-B, Data-C and so on are open to us.

Data-A then, is an aesthetic in the way I referenced it previously, but its uniqueness comes from the fact that Data-A actually reconciles humanity with Nature to generate a partnership that is specifically tailored for the Anthropocene, as what is critical in this epoch is life itself and humanity and Nature are the only agents that can redirect life on earth towards a sustainable continuity and out of CEGE's grip.

I mean "reconciliation" as in the process of making a mutual enterprise consistent and compatible to the interest of life and all of the creatures that partake of it on Earth.

What else could you imagine would give us a better basis for a partnership at the star of a long migration to the safety of a stable and productive world?

There is however a powerful reason for me to present Data-A as an Anthropocene aesthetic and not much else beyond that, the reason has to do with Holocene culture in various respects, some of which I wish to make clear.

Very early on in my inquiry into human culture I found a deep well of friction between the pillars of academia in their various disciplines, their biggest gift to civility being their ability to agree to disagree. Things where not much better between political and religious persuasions both of them swimming in seas of false claims and unfulfilled promises. I found the media hostage to fixed ideologies, too obedient to power and much to busy searching out intrigues, controversies, scandals, tragedies and war stories to distract the people away from the real cultural issues and objectives regarding the building of a better world.

I mean no disrespect to any of these entities, really, but that is an encapsulation that has thousands of years in the making, it has never been a secret and it is that way because the culture developed that way. That is all.

That is why Data-A is not presented exclusively as a philosophical proposition, as a scientific hypothesis, as a religious revelation, a business proposition or even a work of with literary value and much less as a revolutionary initiative. Data-A is an all-inclusive aesthetic.

The Anthropocene epoch is not a party and CEGE is not a figment of my imagination, We have lost a lot of time tinkering with Holocene notions that have no chance of success in fact we are already late getting started.

I opted instead to present Data-A as art and its aesthetic as the hybrid that it is resulting from the reconciliation between the two oldest information streams and the unification of art and life, a unification that emerged with extraordinary proof in 2014 (more on that later.) It is on that basis that Data-A is, unless I'm corrected otherwise, the first Anthropocene initiative on Earth that at least offers a way forward.

Data-A has a complete global manifesto that was published in full in 2012 that is available for downloading at no cost at www.tiite.com. However, simply stated Data-A art is a global movement that explores a greater role for life itself in assigning meaning to art.

When it is life itself that is in jeopardy, one does not go in search of ideologies one goes out in search of answers and the meaning of what is already out there that we do not have or have not yet comprehended.

That unresolved mystery is life and oddly enough life, better yet Nature, still have undiscovered answers that we need, to make it through the early Anthropocene epoch.

I have endowed Data-A aesthetic with three (3) new principles and two (2) new perspectives that I found embedded in Nature, while I'm sure they are not the last hidden treasures there, I'm sure that they will take us a long ways.

These new cultural instruments will help to upgrade the human cultural context fast enough to were the initial benefits can become a successful defense against CEGE and possibly its total annihilation over time.
Like all new things of course, they will feel awkward and strange at first, although Nature seems to be quite comfortable to use them, in fact I dare think that Nature wouldn't work without them.

Here is a taste of what the principles are:

1. Sufficiency, is a noun meaning "the state or fact of being adequate or enough" however, it is a word that turned out to harbor a profound message for the Anthropocene. So much so that it may become a scientific field on its own right. Briefly, Sufficiency suggests a quantifiable analysis of a condition whose very existence leads to the occurrence of a given event or to the existence of a given

thing. In other words, sufficiency is a measure that indicates the best operative proportions that make something (a galaxy) or someone (a flower) or a mind-object (an idea) whole in design, function, and adaptability to its environment, to adjacent conditions and to its contributing role to the sufficiency of the whole. That is, the galaxy to space and time, the flower to the meadow, the idea to the cultural context and all to the same universe. Why is sufficiency critical for us in the Anthropocene? Because sufficiency will be our guide to establish a sense of proportion to human culture and a quantifiable adequacy to our activity in concert with the sufficiency requirements of life on Earth. Sufficiency in Nature, let's say in a square mile of Amazonian forest for example, houses, feeds and sustains trillions of creatures daily in concert with the world, with the requirements of each creature fulfilled and while contributing to the requirements of all life on Earth and I may add that all of that has happened without producing a single ounce of trash for over two billion years. That is sufficiency and its secrets are now a needed cultural instrument that is at our hand.

2.   Sustainable continuity, is in a way the effect of sufficiency on the stability of

creatures, things and so on, but it also has a profound message for us in the Anthropocene as continuity is a concept that we have somewhat understood in the context of our own human nature and in relation to traditions and other cultural artifacts which are preserved as individual expressions of a given culture. Continuity in nature is more of a principle, in that in the progression of life on Earth, certain features and basic processes (RNA or DNA for instance) are sustained in continuity even if the current recipients of those endowments do not look anything like their ancestral donors. Sustainable continuity is a new Anthropocene principle because we changed the fundamental nature of the planet, its chemistry, its atmospheric make up, its environment, and the historical integrity of the entire biosphere. Sustainable continuity then, is about the systematic tabulation and rigorous analysis of the essential global biota (animals, plants, fungi, microbial and viral) that is absolutely essential to life, as we knew it and the technological requirements needed to sustain them in continuity. There is another side to sustainable continuity and that is also equally critical to the human project, and that is the cultural context of the human species as a whole. In the Holocene we have fought and died by the millions for the differences between ideas and beliefs but we have also climbed to the top of the food chain and became as wise as the culture permitted. That entire story is our cultural context and in the Anthropocene thanks to sufficiency, none of the ideas have to be thrown away, none of them are nonsense or babble, but they are instead essential markers neatly organized in their own place and time, each telling us a chapter about the peculiar history of a species that is finally learning that sustainable continuity of the human spirit will never be complete without all of the pages that make us what we really are, an ever wandering migrating and beautiful species.

3. Integral consciousness is a natural principle that to us, at present, is more of a target goal than it is, say, a plug and play appliance. In the Anthropocene however, that goal is motivated by the fact that Nature is wholly unified and if consciousness is a window for us to see that fact then we should also be able to understand it and to enter nature's unification and to see ourselves from within that context. That target is far from our entry point in the Anthropocene, but the road to it will register the impressions

of our first footprints, as our reconciliation with the world to work in partnership with nature, is indeed an act of integral consciousness. The fact that the advance of CEGE's attack on civilization will make it possible for us to finally see ourselves as a single species whose collaborative effort is the best offence that we have, is indeed another act of integral consciousness. The fact that our partnership with nature is a joint effort to focus on all life on Earth is indeed a grand act of integral consciousness, a bit primitive by universal standards but we have to start somewhere.

As can be appreciated these principles are in their infancy and my view into them is not much different from that of Columbus upon setting foot in the Americas. They are in need of exploration and will produce results that I could have never dreamed of, however their exploration requires at least two more cultural instruments or perspectives, which I will mention next.

1. Critical perspective, this is a natural extension to critical thinking, which like all other human thought, resides within the sphere of our human nature whose cultural context while inspired in part by nature is nonetheless independent from it. Critical Perspective is again a purely Anthropocene artifact emerging to sustain

the aforementioned principles in the global environment in which the events are taking place, at the terrestrial scale to which they belong and within the covenant of a partnership between humanity and the world. Critical perspective may be thought of as a platform from where our critical thinking synthesis jumps off into its global theatre where the terrestrial concerns inform the meaning and value of the reasoned judgments made on behalf of life. Therefore Critical perspective effectively magnifies our "sense" and "meaning" of locality to encompass the self, the immediate surroundings, the national, the international and the global physical and conscious environment, it includes Nature and all life, as an extension of our traditional perception of "home." Such critical perspective should in time, extend beyond the earthly realm to include our solar system, the Milky Way and ultimately the universe as the totality of our conception of life at home.

2. The green path is another Anthropocene aesthetic invention aimed at tying together the history of life on Earth with our own history in a critical perspective where their unification results in a fresh new course for the collective survival of all

living things on Earth, merged on to a common survival path.

It is an imaginary path that also corresponds to the unfolding of Nature through time, a path that is constrained by our specie's best understanding of life based on evidence and reason, ingredients that when blended together with the historical unfolding of our own nature, impels the human urge for the manifestation of meaning and physical creativity to an unprecedented and refined state of global consciousness that may be manifested in real time in the real world as the new relationship unfolds..

Conceptually, the Green-Path is exceptionally simple as a cultural trail into the conscious landscape that defines the physical character of the history of life leading forward into a different world.

The Green-Path opens up for the human imagination the exploration of a level of consciousness which is founded on the synthesis of our combined understanding of the world from the accumulation of contributions to that understanding made by earlier explorers over thousands of years. Add to that the fact that our present understanding of the world comes billions of years after our world became a part of an immensely dynamic and older universe to which we owe our place of provenance or origin.

The Green-Path invites our concept of integration to expand its inclusion capability to acknowledge the known diversity of human ideas about everything as the real context of human nature. Further, that expanded notion allows our human nature to experience the physical reality that we, humans, in spite of our diversity are indeed members of the same species (Homo sapiens,) and that our species is related and shares the history and splendor of life, with the diversity of all other life on Earth. Just imagine that this small step in integration is sufficient to open the door for our conscious to integrate itself with the vast diversity of the universe in which we are but a tiny though priceless speck.

Data-A as an Anthropocene aesthetic, is a response to a real crisis in real time at a moment in history when we personally and collectively should do everything possible to secure this beautiful planet, from the ravishes of human innocence in whatever form.

Data-A aesthetic therefore opens up a dialog that greatly expands the human conscious landscape where our presence in the world is to acquire distinctions never before imagined such as becoming the first species in the history of planet Earth to evolve to be able to partner with the very nature and processes that gave the species origin and thereby take a role in the continuous procession of life itself, as a direct agent in its direction and its future.

The benefits do not stop there however, as the dialog and application of these cultural instruments are in themselves the upgrade package for a greater cognitive capacity, breaking thereby, the 50,000 thousand or so year old cognitive barrier, that prevented us from seeing the Anthropocene world on the horizon at the beginning of the industrial age.

Furthermore, an increased cognitive capacity that can observe life from that higher level of comprehension will not be too far from being able to participate directly in the perceptive beat of all life in the planet. That is a capacity where all life is to be perceived more intimately than we have managed to perceive our own existence at present and even beyond into degrees of intimacy with the Earth process itself.

That key; my dear readers, will unlock a generous new number of the mysteries that are still off limits to humanity but whose possession will prove to be a critical endowment not only for the campaign against CEGE but also for the recovery of life in the Anthropocene.

Let us keep in mind, that life has always been this planet's best choice; let us see that we evolve culturally to see, that the choice stands.

"Culture of Peace"

Chapter VII
A culture of peace

Now for the easiest and most remarkable quiz in the history of civilization:
What was the one culture that never emerged during the Holocene epoch or indeed ever in the history of the human species?

You may be surprised to know that the answer is "a culture of peace." Hard as it seems an in spite of the millions of people who over millennia died for various noble causes and that now rest in peace; never able to tell us what that is.

Peace is one of those conscious artifacts that humanity has been talking about for as long as war has existed, however, it has been a goal as remote as the Andromeda galaxy, at least from human reach and the actualization of peace as something in the physical world that cannot be confused with anything else.

I grant that inner peace is just as popular and attainable perhaps by everybody in various degrees, as peace within the human mind can be anything you say is peace, but exteriorly we have yet to see it. Why is that?

While I'm sure you have your own opinion on the matter, your opinion would be right, because all we have are opinions about peace and nothing of real substance to show for them. There must be thousands of peace organizations with various missions that on close inspection, turn out to be valuable war mediation entities doing extraordinary work in the name of peace.

I will however, ask a question and volunteer an answer as to why peace was never really needed, the answer will provide a reason, which becomes ever more clear when seen from an Anthropocene perspective.

Why would we need something like peace when war has and is still doing so well for us? Keep in mind that, that is a question asked from within the Holocene mentality.
The answer from an Anthropocene perspective is of course that we don't!

Why would you need something like peace when civilization itself was built around war, funded by war over thousands of years and up until today, when war is still the largest employer in the planet with stakes and direct interest for its supplies, in just about every industry known to civilization. Oh really!

Really, war is what it is because over the millennia war has developed a culture all of its own, a culture of war that has permeated every aspect of human activity, a culture of war that is deliberately perpetuated from cradle to grave and that is omnipresent in all human affairs.

That is why a concept of peace with a physical presence has been absent all along and also why the idea of peace has been no more than a curious mind-object lurking in the shadows of war without a significant physical presence of its own.

By way of illustration, think of a time during the reign of the dinosaurs and of their mighty presence in the world, whilst tiny mammals scurried about underground meekly surviving in the shadows of the lumbering giants.

Then, an asteroid changed all that and wiped out the giants and the little guys emerged from the shadows to evolve to rule the world.

Thankfully, in the Anthropocene there is no need to wipe out war, not when our biggest battle with CEGE is about to unfold and humanity will have to put to work everything we have learned in 5,000 years about warfare and more; much more.

A culture of peace therefore is as we have just seen a culture that could not have risen in any other place or time but here in the Anthropocene epoch. However, a culture of peace like anything else in the physical world requires a design, a structure, an infrastructure and well-defined purpose and cultural mission.

What we have for peace at the moment are slogans and unrealizable demands for peace that are not much more than pledges to do something that we believe in, but that we do not as yet know how to do.

Just imagine declaring war, without having a military base, a chain of command, weapons, soldiers, mobilization equipment, rations and supplies, specific targets, or even an enemy we can clearly distinguish from a neighbor.

Well, that is what we have been doing for centuries when we demand peace, as if the word peace, itself, when we finally find it, would turn out to be this great ready-made package that contains all of the accouterments of peace.

In my own lifetime when John and Yoko Lennon urged us to "imagine peace" I did not take it as an exercise to imagine a word, but as an invitation to continue to imagine a process with all of the things that it may contain and all of the agents than can make it work.

Incidentally in 1982 I painted a mural titled "Diffusion Billboard Opus 1982" a 1,585' feet long by 8' feet high which I dedicated to John Lennon. Picture the mural standing up next to the Empire

State building and see 200' feet of it projecting over the top of the antenna; now imagine the content of the mural as the thesis which brought me to this moment as I write for you about a culture of peace.

A culture of peace as the key word indicates is a process of, well, "cultivation" from a simple and perhaps unremarkable seed that is to be tended, irrigated and fertilized with fresh ideas as it grows and then gently harvested; its new seeds replanted to secure larger crops until the whole world can grow and consume the fruits of a culture of peace.

That is not far fetched at all, in fact that is the history of war as well, the first bullets where mudballs thrown from slings and you know the rest. How powerful is the reach of the culture of war is evidenced by the largest catalog of documents in the history of writing, by the fact that the history of the human species so far, is a faithful record of the culture of war as our most prominent cultural feature during the Holocene epoch.

A culture of peace in the Anthropocene epoch is not just a cultural new luxury but also a critical necessity without which the hopes for the survival of civilization are diminished to the point of a lost cause.

In this new world the balance of power does not lay on the one with the most guns but rather on the collective effort engaged by humanity as a single species, where war and peace are the balancing polarities whose combined effect ignites our best offence against CEGE.

The time when war and peace where seen as separate and opposite impulses is now Holocene history. So is the time when the human ambition for world domination depended on the subjugation of our own kind to get all of the toys at the expense of the future of life; those prospects on the face of CEGE are silly at best.

War and peace will come to be seen and not a moment too soon, as opposite polarities of the same survival instrument that may if allowed to function, set human civilization on this new migration path through the new world.

Let me illustrate that point, we are all familiar with the eponymous battery; with it we power anything that requires reliable portable power, from a flashlight to solar automobiles. At one end we have a negative pole, let's call it "war" and at the other end a positive pole, let's call it "peace," let's keep in mind that by themselves they are, well, powerless to do something that only the two polarities in concert can do.

In that proposition, the inescapable truth is that none of the polarities are more or less important than the other, that they balance power in such way so as to deliver a maximum and uniform charge to a target, whatever the target may be, a civil society in a livable world, or an all out attack against CEGE.

That is why a culture of peace is such a breath of fresh air in the Anthropocene, because peace does not have to quarrel with war, they just finally unite their effects to charge civilization to illuminate the migration route to a better survival strategy for civilization.

The contrast between that proposition and the former is inimitable, just consider that while on one hand, it is true that war has done a lot of things over the millennia, one cannot possibly miss to notice that no matter what the attending circumstances are, war, has always involved needless death and destruction in fact that is war's best known avatar.

On the other hand, peace is just a word that shows up to the burial services of the victims from both sides, dressed, as a white banner and carried forward to express condolences and reparation that sponsor a truce; meanwhile as it happened so many times, while that is going on, new of follow up plans and supplies are being arranged for the next war.

The propitiousness of the emergence of a culture of peace at the beginning of our journey in the Anthropocene cannot be underestimated nor can the importance of another unique characteristic that comes on board to further secure our passage.

I'm talking about Nature and the fact, that because of the new covenant between human nature and Nature at large, their unification makes peace to be a joint effort with life on Earth on behalf of life itself on Earth.

That means that, the powerful battery that I described before will learn to use its energy to light our way through the battlefields against CEGE an on to the unification of our species as the self appointed custodian of life on Earth.

I'm sure, that you have by now noticed that I'm presenting a proposition for a culture of peace as if all of humanity was already at peace with each other and rearing to go, to begin to restore civilization and the world's environment.

I know quite well that that is not the case and that at present with all of the social, religious, political and economic unrest, I would be hard press to find anyone who will actually take the time to care, perhaps not about what I'm saying here, but about the possibility that there is a way out of this predicament.

The sad truth however, is that it is all going to get worse and it has, but that is the strength of the proposition of a culture of peace because we humanity cannot avoid the fact that war on its own has nothing to offer but more death, suffering and destruction and that we have been killing each others children long enough and for all the wrong reasons.

We all know that in the face of the challenges that are already at our door, bracing for war is the right thing but to continue killing each other is the wrong war; CEGE is already doing that with impunity and sparing no one. I mean no one.

Culture is at the root of our global dilemmas and culture is the only agency that has a chance to help us to remedy them. A culture of peace is therefore not as simple as one may suspect, in fact, it is a complex architecture that we can build now that we know how to begin and with cultural instruments that can help us to begin to build it now.

There is another aspect, which I will mention on closing this chapter and it is that a culture of peace as described here is merely a kernel in a much larger discussion about peace and its power to help redirect the direction of human culture.

A culture of peace that is based on the same fundamental Anthropocene cultural improvements mentioned here, is just like all of the other cultural patterns that are and can be adopted by different local global cultures, cultures that in terms, give their culture of peace their own local flavor as it is adopted into their own unique and national cultural context.

As we are now a global civilization, it would be very difficult to cultivate a culture of peace without having a global pattern from which the individual nations can source as it where, the culture of peace seedlings of the same original cultural pattern of peace that is established globally for our species own use.

Therefore, a global pattern of a culture of peace would have to be established first and that is the subject of the next chapter, where we will come face to face with an even bolder proposition that took the better part of a half a century to dream up and put together, but that is proudly a theory for a global culture of world peace.

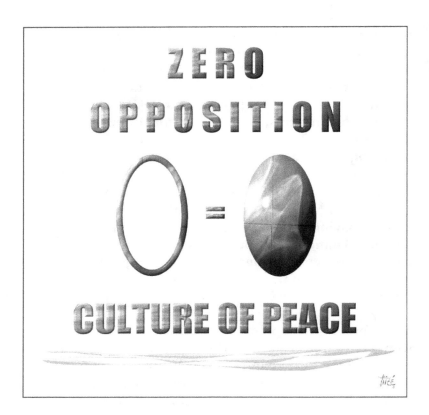

"Initial Conditions"

Chapter VIII
Approaching and declaring a general theory for a culture of world peace

There has been a tendency or even perhaps a norm in the Holocene epoch or at least for most of the length of the history of civilization to describe peace, or now days, world peace as an ideal of freedom, happiness, peace and nonviolence, all nouns of words whose actual realization are as vague as the ideal of world peace.

Further, we have pursued those ideals by appealing to a system of governance or by virtue of several theories that are stratified in other ideologies whose aim is the attainment of more abstract ideals that have not being realized either or at least in a significant way as to get humanity any closer to a realized experience of anything like world peace. Why is that so?

Well, there are many contributing reasons and many complex issues that prevent those ideals to have a physical presence in the human experience, but, not if you look at that landscape of ideals from an Anthropocene perspective, specially now that we know that these shortcomings are the direct product of an incomplete cultural context, that cannot process an idea such as peace or world peace, without the new cultural instruments that can allow the culture to be able to process them to arise.

That is why human civilization does not have a cultural experience that can be called peace and the reason is that peace or extensible world peace to exist, would have to be a culture all of its own and not just an ideal; as it is at present.

Just imagine the inverse and let's describe war as an ideal of battle, conquest, subjugation and acquisition of power through the use of force and then try to picture the realization of that experience without having a culture of war complete with all of the necessary attributes that are unique to warfare.

Therefore we know that the key needed for humanity to open the door to the experience of peace or world peace and all of its desirable attributes, is a realized culture of peace within the national cultural context of each nation and a culture of world peace as the fountain from which all of the nations of the world may obtain the raw material from a global common and fundamental pattern to construct their own version of peace.

By now, you might have noticed that a culture of world peace takes precedence to the national or local experience of a culture of peace. Well, there is a powerful reason for that too.

Even though, we humanity, remain largely influenced by a local frame of reference from which we acquire identity, language and culture in general. Humanity in the Anthropocene epoch may and will still cling to those local, regional and national cultural influences that gave character to their cultural identity during the Holocene. However at the start of our journey through this new Anthropocene world we are a global civilization and our sense of locality must now expand to embrace without any cultural loss and a definite gain, the reality that at a terrestrial level every place in the planet is local to the earth and that fact therefore, constitutes the new boundary to our conception of local.

No less important is the fact that the current global human civilization is made up of members of the same species and therein we have a critical message about ourselves and that is, that the culture of war as it exists throughout the world comes from a long way back in time and therefore, shares the same fundamental principles, no matter what the modern interpretation of its roots are today.

What I'm saying is, that the culture of war was born way before the advent of civilization in fact its roots may go as far back as the early hominids or even further. That is speculation of course but one cannot avoid the thought in light of evidence indicating warfare amongst chimpanzees, and primate violent encounters over territory or for the claim and possession of fruit or other food resources.

If that is taken into account, then it is quite likely that the rudiments of war came with us out of Africa and that what ever we have done with that first seed of war, as we populated the entire world and up to this moment in the age of nuclear warfare, we are still planting and growing war from descendants of that original seed.

Now, going back to a culture of world peace, we also have to establish that first seed from which a culture of peace will emerge and develop into the more robust culture of world peace. To do so, we have to establish first, the initial conditions whereby the culture can come into existence and thereby obtain that first seed.
That initial seed will provide us with the first rudiments or first principles, or better yet with its elemental roots from which all of the attributes that go along with the culture are to follow.

What I'm saying is, that the culture of peace has to enter through the same door that the culture of war came into human culture and that is because the roots will have to be absolutely compatible in origin to the roots of a culture of war; that is absolutely critical.

Let me explain that last point a bit further; while it is impossible to go back to the day and circumstances in which organized warfare was invented, perhaps in Uruk (present day Iraq) some 5,000 years ago, a little bit of reverse engineering could do the trick for peace providing that the initial conditions are matched as closely as possible.

I worked on this problem for over a decade before the astonishingly simple answer popped up, not just to my surprise, but to my embarrassment for the time spent looking for it.

It so happens that if the initial conditions that gave the culture of war a beginning, could also be utilized to give the culture of world peace its beginning as well, we would in fact create a parallel culture that although 5,000 years or more younger than the other, would nonetheless be constructed from the same impulse and despite of their age difference and development, it would actually work because the fundamental initial state has not really evolved, what has evolved is the culture that was born out of it; in that sense, a match of the initial conditions is a match what ever their difference in age.

So what was that astonishingly simple answer? Are you ready?

The initial conditions that determined the beginning of a culture of war to take place, where, a complete absence of opposition, to the idea of war itself.

That was all? Yes it was a complete absence of opposition to the idea of war, which initiated the culture of war.

Today we can call that a singularity in the parlance of mathematics or a perfect genesis from the Greek, origin or creation.

That apparently simple state of non-opposition to the idea of what became this exuberantly complex culture of war started perhaps the way the universe itself began from a state of non-opposition to its existence.

Anyhow if we think about it, we can see that from that moment on, a process was initiated and soon after, a unique structure began to take form as the energies involved began to organize the simple rules of attack and defense, the development of weapons the creation of the soldier, the chain of command and so on. The rest as they say is history.

The same applies for the beginning of a culture of world peace and as we will see later on, a working model at a global scale is already under construction.

In this chapter you may find yourself at the genesis of an idea, which is emerging in the Anthropocene world, hopefully in time to reunite humanity with itself as a single species and to help reunite humanity with the world. To place life itself on the mantle of existence so that together we may a stand against the effects of our innocent adolescence as a species and recover this wonderful water planet, from the condition in which our children are inheriting this world to a world where a culture of war and a culture of peace allied their charges to create a culture of life in continuity, for all of the creatures who contribute to its existence.

What follows is the complete text of my approach to a general theory for a culture of world peace.

APPROACHING

And

DECLARING

A GENERAL THEORY

FOR

A CULTURE OF WORLD PEACE

By:

Tiité Baquero

2014

Approaching and declaring a General Theory for a Culture of World Peace

This work on peace is dedicated to the memory of the millions of people who gave their lives in the pursuit of peace throughout the entire history of human civilization; their bodies laid the path that lead to this remarkable moment.

It is also important to acknowledge with my deepest respect the myriads of contributing material from thinkers of all known subjects over the many thousands of years whose insights provided the guidelines that made this work on peace possible.

I would be remiss if do not echo my eternal gratitude to Nature whose reservoir of wisdom I have been privileged to glance and for the few secrets which I borrowed to give to humanity as cultural instruments which may ease our way back to the world.

The concept of peace is probably one of the oldest abstract ideas to have entered the cultural context of civilization thousands of years ago. Although it is also probable that the concept of peace dates back even further perhaps to early humans or hominids at the dawn of abstract thought.

That may be hard to prove, however, the fact that the idea of peace has been the constant companion of war for at least 5,000 years of recorded history is a more relevant piece of data to at least make a case for the notion that peace exists almost purely as an abstract illusion, an illusion that is maintained alive by the brutality of war against our own kind and the deeply rooted stream of violence that runs in the cultural context of humanity.

The idea of a theory of peace has never really found footing outside of its personal, interpersonal and international relationships or as solicitor for human rights, justice, or as mediator between warring partners. Those efforts though salutary have never dealt with an independent idea of peace other than peace as a shadow of war, or more commonly as a placeholder for a concept of peace that as it happens, is buried deep within a culture of war.

One could rightfully suggest that many of the extant theories of peace fall short of peace, likely because, in a civilization where the greatest social, political, economic and industrial incentive is war, an independent idea of peace would be a nuisance to a power based way of life.

The notion of no more war favored by many generations, as noble as it may seem, is a notion which if it was to be acted upon, would produce a kind of peace which could not be sustained in the real world for more than a day.

The decree of no more war, in actual practice, would begin with an unbearable loss of employment numbering in the billions of people without jobs, as war in the fullest sense is the biggest employer of human activity par none.

That is in a nutshell why current theories of peace cannot possibly succeed beyond mediation and proportional management of conflict within the political interest of the parties involved.

One must grant that the issues involved in keeping the idea of peace alive in the theatre of human activity are complex and those involved in the practice are responsible for what ever good can be said about humanity in its search for a tangible and quantifiable concept of peace.

The prospects for a viable theory of peace emerging from within a cultural context so rooted in violence as we have seen, were never too good; the emergence of a theory of peace requires a unique set of circumstances where a new level of necessity would again provide the door through which a concept of a culture of world peace may be added to the human cultural context in order to address such need.

This is what I mean. Up until now, there was no point in having a culture of peace and much less the contemplation of a culture of world peace, the question being; peace – what ever for?
Peace as an illusion works well and does not upset the status quo, so why bring in an unnecessary complication that is best left alone.

In other words, a passive campaign like "Imagine Peace" for example, is a cultural exercise that keeps the idea of peace alive but does not require a structured physical presence because the only requisite is to imagine peace.

The approach to a general theory for a culture of world peace outlined here is surfacing from a most unexpected source, coupled together with a most surprising motivation and in the form of a response to a totally unforeseen necessity, which is arising at the beginning of a whole new chapter in the history of humanity and of planet Earth. Consider that...

- The unexpected source is the arts, even though art has been a faithful contributor to human culture, however, to my knowledge, art has not contributed critical specific material towards the construction of a theory in any given subject, that is until now...(as we will see further on)

- The surprising motivation is that an approach to a general theory for a culture of world peace like the one being advanced here actually emerges to help the culture of war to evolve in order to meet the demands of an entirely new enemy who is already at our front door... (More on that later)

- The totally unforeseen necessity is the onset of the Anthropocene epoch which is the aftermath consequence of all human activity that is shaping a new world which is increasingly growing hostile to life forms like us, while at the same time, its effects are also undermining the integrity of all of our planetary life support systems.

This approach to a general theory for a culture of world peace therefore, surfaces as a response to a landscape of challenges that are among other things, shaping the survival odds for civilization. The theory however, may effectively contribute to the quantity and quality of the human response to a geological epoch where humanity was the principal architect and an epoch for which, humanity is the only force that can counteract the negative effect of all previous human activity. Furthermore, it is in that same landscape of challenges where humanity aided by a culture of world peace may find the incentive to evolve culturally in order to learn how to sustain life on Earth in continuity.

Having presented the previous considerations, how then, is a general theory for a culture of world peace to be couched and what are the fundamental ideas behind it?

It appears that the most fundamental key behind the approach to a general theory for a culture of world peace is embedded in culture itself.

Culture is the basic nucleus, the ideal medium and the conscious environment where an idea such as peace can emerge, take form and flourish as an independent construct in a confluence of ideas existing within the human cultural context.

In such a cultural context all other ideas gravitate around with their own independent meaning and function, however, ideas can be ordained to form a specific chain of relationships when they are attached to a core idea whose principle can serve as the foundation where many ideas can assemble into a definite concept such as world peace.

Therefore, it is imperative, that the approach to a general theory for a culture of world peace be presented in continuation of what human culture has evolved to be at present and up to the boundary where our current cultural context fails or is no longer able to respond to new cultural and environmental demands which never existed before, but, that are occurring at this moment in history.

Beyond that cultural boundary, new cultural instruments will need to be created and put in place, in order to overcome the cultural shortfall or deficit I just mentioned. The effect of the new cultural instruments put in place and in service however, would go on by virtue of their character and results to signal the presence of evolutionary activity in the overall human cultural context.

Allow me to put the last paragraph into perspective; While much debate remains on how we came to be as a species, it is not too soon to accept the notion that regardless of our precise origin, what has been called the human experiment or the human project, began with very few ideas and essential tools like sticks and stones which over a period of many a millennia, evolved into an arsenal of ideas and tools which we effectively used to create an independent nature of our own, a nature that was good enough to engineer a number of civilizations, to discover, use and apply technology to create a number of scientific miracles, a vast quantity of nightmarish weapons of warfare and to eventually conquer the planet.

Beyond that often overlooked but well known part of our history, lies the reality of our current condition which indicates that, given the environmental state of the planet and the current state of uncertainty attending human civilization, we are staring at conditions that give way to ever increasing evidence that our cultural context is incomplete. That is, it lacks the instruments needed, to deliver a sustainable civilization or a culture that is capable of arresting the trend of activities, which are placing civilization in jeopardy of collapse along with the rest of life, as we know it.

Those concerns are confirmed by the onset of the Anthropocene epoch, itself the geological boundary that unquestionably attests to the effect of human activity on the planet. Furthermore, our haphazard initial response to its effects provides convincing evidence of our inability to address its challenges and gives visibility to the cultural boundary, which prevents us from doing so.

The Anthropocene epoch is an immensely complex scenario which is revealing itself to be not just as a new world geologically speaking, but also a social nightmare in terms of the effects on human activity stemming from events that were never really foreseen or prepared for by anyone. So much so that, the extent of their impact may in fact, constitute the main trigger for a mass extinction event that was inadvertently unleashed by human civilization.

I therefore, submit to you the previous narrative as a minimal set up, so that on that stage I may articulate an approach to a general theory for a culture of world peace. Undoubtedly, this is a critical moment in history when the presence of world peace can play a pivotal role and when its exploration can be the difference between the success and failure of civilization.

As it turns out, peace or more properly world peace is a component that is missing from the human cultural context and understandably so, because humanity never had a culturally compelling survival reason to institute anything like world peace, at least not until now.

Therefore considering that in the absence of anything resembling world peace, a relevant or serviceable kind of world peace cannot be instituted as an active component of human civilization, that is, until a "culture of world peace" is first put in place, in order to serve as the foundation upon which the kind of experiences that identify the presence of world peace, can be attributed as effects derived from a culture of world peace.

Consider by way of analogy, the case of our culture of war and the way that war makes its effects readily visible and evident to all, as experiences that are undoubtedly derived from a culture of war. Keeping in mind of course, that war itself is already an active and ongoing physical component of human civilization, were world peace is not.

Similarly, world peace has to be seen and experienced as clearly as we can see war, therefore a culture of world peace enters civilization at this time, as an ideal new instrument that may allows us to finally experience the effect of world peace for the first time. A culture of world peace enters human culture pretty much, like Galileo's telescope entered human culture and allowed us to see Jupiter and its moons for the first time and forever opened to human civilization the door to the universe.

Therefore a general theory for a culture of world peace should enter the discourse of human civilization as a cultural instrument which is ideally instituted at a point in human development, were its presence, can be developed to play a distinct role in the human response to the Anthropocene epoch.

One can think of a culture of world peace and of peace itself, as survival links, which have been dormant probably from the start of human culture and prior to the beginning of human civilization, but most assuredly during the last 5,000 years of its history.

The notions of peace that we have sustained in the past have been kept alive as mere dreams and expectations until now. They are notions of peace that have to be awakened and upgraded by necessity in order to repair a flaw caused by the absence of a culture of peace in our activity.

Having said that, we can now begin to frame in a slightly broader sense what a "Culture of World Peace" means

If one can accept the idea that the Anthropocene epoch is the collision point between human activity and the world, that, it is a point where a whole new set of social and environmental conditions come into play, then, it would not be difficult to accept that the idea of world peace is no longer exclusively a human preoccupation but rather, given the nature of the new Anthropocene epoch, a preoccupation for all life on Earth.

Therefore in that context, the idea of a Culture of World Peace is about humanity in a paradigm of peace with itself and by extension humanity in a paradigm of peace with the world*.
* World is used as short hand for all of the processes and all other life forms outside of the purview of human civilization.

A culture of world peace is about the reconciliation of the planet with itself in terms of all life, as the prospects for life as we know it in the environment of the Anthropocene epoch are dismal at best, that is, unless the human response to its many challenges, is issued from a position of unification or of solidarity against its negative effects.

A culture of world peace offers the best chance to unify humanity to mount a formidable collective response against the onslaught of the cumulative effects of past human activity. The Anthropocene epoch is not just the name of a new geological epoch, but it is also the name for a period of time whose environmental content already is one of the most egregious threats to all life in the history of planet Earth.

There is a tendency to think of issues such as global warming, climate change, ocean acidification and so on, in isolation from each other, as if they have different schedules and time scales to act upon the world. The fact is that they are all here, they are all active and interactive with new ones emerging and they are all affecting the world at the same time. Their existence is so evident, that the combined effect of their issues upon the world is precisely what gave origin to the new state of the world that scientists call the Anthropocene epoch.

I have given a name to the cumulative effects of past and current human activity, and I did so, in the absence of any published relevant data, which might have been published in an attempt to link together the cumulative effects of human activity. I have named the monstrosity "CEGE" which is an acronym for COMPOUNDED ENVIRONMENTAL GLOBAL EFFECT.

CEGE anticipates the formal compilation of all the known environmental issues, the known and unknown interactions amongst them and the attempt to account for their single and combined effect upon the Earth's biosphere and lithosphere.

I have distinctively named CEGE to be a creature of the Anthropocene epoch; it is a creature which we, humanity, have not identified as such and likely because the notion relies on a critical perspective of all of the issues examined at a global scale and for which the cultural instruments needed to embrace the nature of CEGE are just emerging here.

Nonetheless CEGE, as conceived here, is likely to enter the dialog of the Anthropocene epoch as a valid cultural device designed to give visibility to the many issues involved. CEGE borrows from our human attraction to myth and monsters to present a visual and perceptive incarnation of the reality that inspired the monstrosity which human activity inadvertently unleashed upon the world, that, dear reader is CEGE.

If the question; what does CEGE has to do with an approach to a general theory for a culture of world peace came up as you read the previous paragraphs, the quick answer is that CEGE has everything to do with it.

So much so in fact that one can argue that the emergence of a culture of world peace at this moment in history may prove to be a dramatic "security measure" for domestic, national, international and indeed global incidents of human conflict, as occasioned by the effects of climate change, diminishing resources, failed crops and new levels of poverty and disease associated with GEGE's complex effect structure.

If up until this moment in time, the idea of world peace has been a passive, contemplative and abstract exercise with not much to offer beyond hope for humanity in the shadows of the power and activity behind the culture of war; that is emphatically not the case anymore.

Rather, this is the moment in time when an active culture of world peace should effectively step up to help transform the idea of world peace from passive to active and from abstract to concrete as a dynamic concept whose time has come.

What the evidence behind the issues behind the Anthropocene epoch suggests is already largely the actual landscape, through which human civilization and the rest of life on Earth are moving through at present. It is also a landscape that demands a level of human cooperation and collectivity that only an evolved idea of peace can help to deliver, since we all know that more of the same would not do.

A culture of world peace is therefore a pre-requisite upon which the idea of world peace materializes and begins to develop. We've always had for some reason, entertained the notion that peace should come already fully formed after some victorious event, that notion is as innocent as would be the expectation that, in the first ancient wars, soldiers used weapons of mass destruction instead of the spears, slingshots and other weapons that archeologists suggested to have been used in early warfare.

Therefore, before the idea of world peace can have a fresh meaning based on an actual experience that can stand as evidence for its existence, there must first be a culture of world peace in place to be able to embrace the experience, make the observation, evaluate the effect to benefit and learn from its results.

It is only then, when a culture of world peace may be defined by its merits as a cultural instrument, which is establishing the foundations for world peace in the real world. From that point on, the idea of world peace may secure an identity, form, function and develop its cultural meaning through its cumulative narrative.

As a culture of world peace develops, its influence is likely to support the reconciliation of human nature with the nature of the world. That reconciliation marks the beginning of what can be thought of as a process whereby the planet and the life on it are reconciling to secure a unified survival strategy a unity that fosters sustainable continuity.

Furthermore, in terms of human consciousness, a culture of world peace is an evolutionary benchmark signaling that human culture has began to evolve to meet its responsibilities to life in a world where human activity has nearly destroyed life, at least life of the sort that supports human existence.

Having said that, we can proceed to establish some of the fundamental framework for a culture of world peace, that is, a culture of world peace has to focus on all life and thus be general and global in nature, that is inclusive of humanity as a single species while also acting and operating in partnership with Nature at a planetary scale.

It therefore becomes clear that a culture of world peace is the organizational agency behind the development of something like world peace, which is itself the effect or consequence of such culture.

Furthermore, a culture of world peace differs from all other previous approaches to world peace in that it is a truly planetary objective rather than civilization's attempt to cope with the effects of human conflict. Instead it becomes a unique characteristic of civilization's first attempt at counteracting the effects of human activity in the Anthropocene epoch.

How then, can we bring all of that together to approach a general theory for a culture of world peace?

To accomplish that, we have to establish a starting point, that is, a point that is without contention with anything ever said or pronounced about peace or any previous approach to world peace. I'm referring to a starting point where all of the attributes and inventions that constitute the basis for the cultural improvements that are needed to support the new theory, are at a state of potential activity where their possible effects are embraced as a likely probability and where all other considerations can be acknowledged thereafter.

In other words a culture of world peace must have initial conditions that begin at ZERO – zero is defined here as the base for any incremental quantity with a positive or negative value.

Therefore, the principal assumption to approach a formal theory for a Culture of World Peace is…

That the cultural narrative for world peace must begin at a zero point.

The fundamental requirements for a Zero point beginning of a culture of world peace are:

1. The Zero point has to be secured in a global context.
2. The context must be substantiated by a worldwide sample of a human collective.
3. The collective must be representative of the entire human species as it occurs in its current global geographical distribution.
4. The human collective must represent the national identity and culture of all the existing nations tallied in the sample.
5. A true global context must be considered when by extension the human collective embraces the existence of all other life coexisting with humanity in the unique ecological niches that as a whole comprise the diversity of life on Earth represented in the potential culture of world peace.

That Hypothesis is then tested by experiment, the experiment is designed in such a way as to maintain the integrity of the fundamental requirements and go on to supply the evidence needed to establish a "zero" point foundation for the culture of world peace which in terms will go on to prove or disprove the theory.

The experiment:
In October 30, 2002 the Worldwide Peace Marker Project collective (WPMP collective) was launched from Rubicond Park in the City of Cape Coral, Florida. The project now entering its twelve-year has already acquired sufficient data to predict a positive proof for the zero point hypotheses.

Here is how such a complex but elegant experiment is laid out...

The experiment is conducted as a work of art, in fact a new art was developed to suit the experiment's requirements, the new art is called Data-A (see manifesto www.tiite.com) itself an information-based aesthetic which is capable to secure the experiment from bias and contamination from any known preexisting ideology or motive other that the ideas behind the experimental requisites needed to establish a zero point foundation for a culture of world peace.

Accordingly, in the experiment's criteria, it was established that the integrity of zero, has to be preserved from any narrative describing motive, purpose, directive or destination that would add up value or quantity to the zero proposition while also preserving the potential value of motive, purpose, directive and destination. That was accomplished by formulating a question, which could carry the fundamental content of the hypothesis while adding no value to its zero point of observation.

The question is: Do you oppose the idea of world peace?

That question is asked to each of the 198 artists who collaborate in the work in the role of Artist Ambassadors to each of the 198 nations selected for the "Worldwide Peace Marker Project collective" (see www.wpmpcollective.com)

Understandably, the prevailing answer to "do you oppose the idea of world peace" is "NO" as shown by the response from the artists Ambassadors from 33 nations who have already joined the Worldwide Peace Marker Project collective.

Therefore it can be assumed that if 198 artists representing 198 nations are united in their non-opposition to the idea of world peace, a global non-opposition consensus is reached. Having voiced that choice, the pledge is made physical by embodying it in the shape of a Peace Marker (a sculptural object placed in each nation,) which overall constitute a worldwide installation of points of peace which cannot be described as anything but an array of markers around the world materializing the presence of a zero point structure, which signals the beginning for a global culture of world peace. A global non-opposition to the idea of world peace thereby allows the idea to emerge as a point of peace distributed throughout the entire world.

That is dramatic evidence for the hypotheses and for the zero point start of the narrative of world peace, as the global presence of a non-opposition to the idea of world peace is in fact the first positive step in the creation of a culture of world peace as sustained by its 198 Artist Ambassadors, who, by merely greeting each other in non-opposition to the idea of world peace, generate over 39,000 communication lines about world peace which effectively span the entire world.

That constitutes evidence for the initial conditions and the emergence of a global culture of world peace from a zero point origin and constitutes convincing empirical proof for the theory.

The cultural narrative of world peace therefore begins there and may be seen to grow incrementally. In addition, the history of its very simple beginning, together with the actors involved and the aesthetic of its presentation, initiates the narrative, which becomes the very first page of the history of world peace on earth.

It must be noted that the experiment as a work of art is a work in progress, yet, it is not to soon to appreciate that Data-A aesthetic can generate an elegant, simple and minimal model of an approach to a theory for a culture of world peace, where a zero point of origin becomes the genesis for a visible, global, active, dynamic and experiential idea of world peace.

World peace is therefore to be born out of a global non opposition to its existence and it comes into existence as a planetary event whose province, function and outlook is life itself and where its concerns, are those of cultivating a culture of world peace that is serviceable to our response to the other planetary event in progress, namely the Anthropocene epoch.

I have described the initial conditions that give origin to a culture of world peace and subsequently to the birth of an independent idea of world peace. However grand that might be, it is in fact just the beginning.

An approach to a general theory for a culture of world peace also requires that the newly born idea of world peace enters the real world arena and establish its role and relationship to human culture and human culture's relationship with the rest of life and to the planet itself.

At first sight that would seem a nearly impossible task for a just born idea of world peace, but, not if it is born endowed with cultural attributes that make possible the adaptation of the idea of world peace to the global context of the environment in which it is born.

Therefore a general theory for a culture of world peace must contain a number of fundamental attributes, which allow the emerging idea of world peace to begin to...

1. Integrate with the existing notions of peace in human culture. That means that world peace as it emerges, does not have to displace any previous notions of peace, rather it validates their existence against a larger ideological background upon which even war is propped up to service at a whole new level of warfare and against a real new formidable enemy as the one embodied in CEGE.
2. World peace should be able to provide a cultural bridge between human culture and the culture of all other life as a natural

discourse of diversity and adaptation.
That means that peace would no longer
be the exclusive province and pursuit of
humanity but a new paradigm concerned
with the integrity of all life from which the
idea of world peace derives its new
cultural context

3. World peace should be able to unify 1 and
   2 into a global context in which the
   planetary processes are a vital part of the
   world peace equation as their unification
   with 1 and 2 sustains the highest
   expectations and true meaning of world
   peace.
4. World peace in those terms should be able
   to contribute effectively to mount a
   formidable response to the challenges to
   life, posed by the Anthropocene epoch.
5. A culture of world peace should be able to
   become an ongoing beacon for the
   sustainable continuity of the new
   relationships which world peace sets-off
   on behalf of life on Earth.

It follows that the fundamental attributes that
drive the actions 1 through 5 just described, are
derivative from the application of a number of
new cultural instruments introduced by Data-A
(see Data-A manifesto www.tiite.com) which are;
the three (3) new fundamental principles plus the
(2) general perspectives.

Therefore, the second assumption to approach a formal theory for a culture of world peace is... That a culture of world peace as proposed here is a phenomenon that is unique to the Anthropocene epoch and that its occurrence should constitute a trigger for fresh cultural evolution in the human species.

The worldwide Peace Marker Project as described in "A Global Work of Art" provides a view of the project as a hypothesis for the formation of a theory for a culture of world peace acting as a test ground for the fundamental ideas driving its design and direction.

It must be noted that continuous evaluation of the ideas involved has generated adjustments, improvements and new data altogether. The project's immediacy to life, all life, makes it a work in progress subject to more than human evaluation as conclusive evidence has surfaced to support the thesis. Most prominent amongst, is the elimination of the gap between art and life. The new evidence though largely foundational, does clear the way for the reconciliation of Human nature and Nature at large, (see 2014 Earth Gallery One update www.tiitebaquero.com)

As with all theories, an approach to a general theory of a "Culture of World Peace" should be able to make testable and replicable predictions.

Therefore based upon the material disclosed here and its additional reference material, I can comfortable predict that, even as the work is still a work in progress one can already see the appearance of a tangible proof, physical presence and narrative consistent with a culture of world peace and consequently, the long awaited idea of world peace will emerge from such culture to be a distinct cultural instrument on behalf of life and particularly in support of a human presence in the Anthropocene epoch.

Declaring a General Theory for a Culture of World Peace

There is a huge gap between traditional ideas about peace and the reality that suggests that peace is (other than efforts for inner peace) an as yet to be attained urge or impulse that remains largely a mental exercise, which also lacks a widely accepted fundamental definition or a well defined quantitative mechanism that can anchor the idea of peace to the reality of the world.

While many theories of peace exist such as; the peace war game in Game theory, democratic peace, theory of active peace, the many peaces theory and Trans-rational peace to name a few. None have been able to be translated into anything that approaches a general theory which can serve as a basket for those individual approaches to peace and the many others who focus on peace but can't reconcile the many variables into a larger concept of peace where their assumed values are or can be seen as contributing characteristics to a general theory.

A general theory for a culture of world peace is formulated here, arguably for the first time in human history. It is a theory, which comes as the result of a 57-year-old quest to understand the idea of peace, motivated by a desire to contribute a mechanism by which that ancient idea of peace may be translated into a physical reality.

The theory is formulated within a cultural framework because the data studied for this purpose, kept pointing toward Peace as being a human invention created to compensate for the absence of an older and more fundamental survival arrangement common to all life and more related to tranquility, than to the ideal harmonic occurrence that we continue to expected to surface in the absence of war.

Therefore the idea of peace is perhaps better understood as an extension of an older natural urge or impulse which humanity included in its cultural matrix during the development of the unique survival strategy we now understand as human nature, a nature which stands independent of Nature at large.

Briefly explained; it follows that in Nature at large, tranquility is a companion of violence if one interprets violence as the injurious force used in the exchange of taking one life to feed one other in the struggle for survival, that is typical of all life and tranquility, as the state of normalcy that exists in the intervals.

In human nature, however, the nature of the struggle for survival has deviated from a simple struggle to live, to a complex struggle for power and dominance over our own kind, its aim is not generally balanced by mutual exchange of life giving resources but an aim somewhat obsessed by mutual annihilation.

Establishing those fundamental differences was a key to open the door to a theory for a culture of world peace and to the realistic expectations that, in establishing a culture of world peace, humanity can finally begin to discover the benefits of a companion to war (rather than a shadow) at a moment in history when war against a formidable enemy to all life like CEGE is at our front door and the knowledge that only peace can orchestrate the level of unity required from us as a single species to effectively combat CEGE.

While war and peace have historically and culturally being assigned the role of opposites and their existence dependent on the absence of one or the other, the circumstances that I just described effectively eliminate that requisite of their existence in the absence of its opposite and begin to look a lot more like their predecessors in the natural model of tranquility and violence as mutual companions.

War and peace therefore can coexist in the inescapable paradigm of the Anthropocene epoch in a relation that is bound to last thousands of years.

It follows that culturally speaking and considering peace as an idea coexisting with war which is endowed with physical consequences, peace, is a concept appearing quite late in the human cultural stage, perhaps some 5,000 years or more behind the establishment of war as a direction with a developing culture to support its aims and expectations.

Nothing demonstrates this point more dramatically than the existence of tens of thousands of written works on the history of war and not one credible and comprehensive written work on the history of peace in circulation anywhere in the world.

It follows that peace must issue forth from a culture of peace, however as the game has changed from local contingencies of tribal or fairly large social groups with distinct identities, geographical holdings and cultural persuasions throughout the planet, a general theory for a culture of world peace would also have to factor a global scale and aim to be able to embrace the entire species for its common denominator, hence a General theory for a culture of world peace.

It must be admitted that peace poses a number of problems that have until now appeared to be insurmountable, largely because it has never been clear just how to begin or how to proceed from there and which cultural instruments may provide the necessary support. In fact, it is not really known for lack of available credible data, whether peace is really desired by humanity outside of its imaginary framework. I certainly hope we do, however, that notion of course, may go a long way in explaining why we still do not have a realized idea of peace.

That gives rise to a critical question; why is it that peace has remained unrealized?

I can now suggest an answer, which, I find indispensable prior to a presentation of my formal theory for a culture of world peace.

Peace has remained an unrealized idea primarily because necessity has never placed a strong enough demand on humanity to act upon a cultural urge to pursue peace with a resolve similar to the one with which humanity has pursued a culture of war for at least the past 5,000 years.

Now at this moment in history, the onset of the Anthropocene epoch has made the demand real enough, gravely critical and so a theory like this one had to emerge and to make predictions that are so peace like that even war will have to take notice, as war's own survival and stability is also thereby secured, perhaps secured longer than the finite expectations on its current course can predict. War will be required to persist, humanity is just going to recalibrate war's motivation rethink its service to the world and that is precisely why a general theory for a culture of world peace enters history at this junction, to assist in that process.

So, what does a general theory for a culture of world peace has to say for itself?

Well, the most prevalent consideration about the theory is that its occurrence is a true Anthropocene phenomenon, which is to say that this theory would not have made sense at any other time in the history of humanity.

A general theory for a culture of world peace is emerging at the same time that the reasons for its utility are emerging; history has shown that a culture of war also emerged at a time when the reasons for its utility emerged.

Similarly, a theory for a culture of world peace enters the human stage accompanied by a challenge in the shape of a mass extinction event in which humanity is not excluded, but in which humanity is the only actor that can arrest its progress.

That challenge requires that humanity work together as a single species and a culture of world peace is the only agent that can unite, bond and keep humanity together, on course and focused on the big prize, life on Earth, through the Anthropocene epoch.

In that context, the theory proposes:

1. That the general theory for a culture of world peace is about a paradigm of humanity at peace with itself and by extension humanity at peace with the world. It is a theory of the unification of life on earth on behalf of its sustainable continuity in the Anthropocene epoch.
2. That a culture of world peace can emerge from nothing and take hold globally with a minimal presence that is subject to exponential growth by virtue of its utility as an Anthropocene cultural instrument. (WPMP collective will be offered as proof)

3. That peace is a direct result of the culture of world peace and that world peace is the overall effect that is observable by humanity in the general objective to a collective solidarity to all life on earth.
4. That peace at a conscious level and peace as a physical expression are functions of the same urge or impulse for tranquility that is common to all life on Earth.
5. That peace as a motivation to human well-being should be the common individual and collective aim of all of humanity as a single species, supported by all of civilization's organizational institutions such as government, the sciences, religion (as a mystical experience) industry and the media.
6. That peace no longer has to come into play in the absence of war but, rather, war and peace are active sides of the same human survival equation. In that equation war engages the Anthropocene enemy CEGE and peace provides the cultural support for war's global engagement with that enemy.
7. That a culture of world peace is an instrument of conservation of all life and as such the fundamental culture and unique expressions of human and other life forms must be preserved and be allowed to transition into the new world of the Anthropocene where their sufficiency

will adapt or transform their identity to
suit the new environment.

8. The general theory for a culture of world
peace may be considered overall as a
transitional cultural instrument between
the end of a period of cultural evolution in
the Holocene epoch and the beginning of
a new period of cultural evolution in the
Anthropocene epoch.

What does the general theory for a culture of
world peace predict?

Initially the theory makes the following
predictions:

1. The theory predicts that world peace can
be a real and quantifiable fact, as its
presence emerges with the confirmation
of the proof and its initial measure.
Therefore the culture emerges with an
effect, which can only be calculated as
peace and thus peace enters human
reality.

2. That the WPMP collective proof provides
not only the foundations for the culture
itself and our first glimpse into an
anatomy for peace, but, also the first
verifiable signs of a cultural evolutionary
event that is specifically triggered by the
arrival of world peace in tandem with the
Anthropocene epoch.

3. That the fledging culture of world peace will immediately begin to transform awareness of critical issues into preliminary designs of practical and doable solutions under the auspice of the first evidence supporting a global collective as provided by the proof.

4. That the global collective fostered by the WPMP collective proof, solidifies and substantiates the prospects for humanity to embrace a "single species state of unity" to become the bastion or stronghold from where human civilization can mount a unified response to CEGE, the Anthropocene menace.

5. That the culture of world peace opens up a window into a single species state of unity dramatized by the Ambassadors and the Peace Markers on the WPMP collective proof does constitute a precondition for the reconciliation between humanity and the world, the proof just previews an instance of that possibility at a global scale.

6. That the presence of a culture of world peace can greatly attenuate conflict and conflict resolution between human actors by virtue of the effects stemming from the single species state of unity, whose solidarity to the global Anthropocene challenge lessens the urgency of many conflicts as the focus is shifted to the

preservation of life. It follows the conflict dictum of the Anthropocene called the "4No's,"that is; "No air-No water-No life-No victory"

7. The theory predicts that given the overwhelming disparity between the power of CEGE and a largely unprepared civilization to engage in battle, against this most formidable enemy of all time and further, knowing that the best defense can be organized by the military forces of the world, the world can engage in direct combat with CEGE, as a result, the Arms Industry will undergo an unprecedented renaissance as the world's military is refitted for battle and a new generation of weapons emerge to arm new generations of soldiers whose charge is nothing less than the balance of life on Earth.

8. The theory predicts that a culture of world peace in its support of the war against CEGE and its focus on all life should also foster an unprecedented economic revival as governments and industries refit the infrastructure of the entire civilized world. The potential economic impact is as incalculable as the cultural impact of a civilization rebuilding its world together in the presence of a culture of world peace.

9. The theory predicts that under the auspice of a culture of world peace, humanity can indeed preserve the marvelous character of their diversity and that their extension to embrace the reality of their being expressions of the same species is a great asset. That is because as each culture is challenged by the Anthropocene world, their adaptive process is supported collectively while each culture defines their own sufficiency in the new world.

10. That governance within a culture of world peace, aided by the cultural instruments which come with it, conveys an alliance of mutuality in purpose, were political persuasions may react to the effects of the Anthropocene with a lessened burden of conflict and a greater global focus on the offensive against CEGE. Further, the social, political and economic interest of each nation state in benefiting from a new war as it always has will be able to better manage the old barriers between unattainable promises and real time recovery models sponsored by the culture and its world peace by-product.

11. The theory predicts that the impact of the world peace equation on the sciences should be remarkable, particularly as the cultural instruments introduced by Data-A aesthetics are explored and refined

further. It will become abundantly clear to the academic disciplines of the world, that the Anthropocene epoch is much more than a mirror upon which, human thought may contemplate the state of its incompleteness, but, it is also a fresh window through which everything that has been said here beckons their vision to the repair, construction and maintenance of a new world.

12. That the impact of a culture of world peace and the appearance of a realized concept of world peace on media and communications will be tremendous as peace becomes news and its evolution becomes the great new story for a whole new kind of media and for generations of new correspondents. Theirs is the beat of a species in transition from a Holocene state of mind to an Anthropocene state of mindfulness, of collectivity, of response to great survival odds, of reconciliation with the world. Theirs is the coverage of the Great War for life on Earth against CEGE. Theirs is the first global narrative for the first ever coverage of the history of peace on Earth as humanity begins to build a new world.

13. A general theory for a culture of world peace, as its "general" character suggests, pertains directly to all persons, groups, organizations and communities

with a peace mission. Therefore is easy to predict that as the proof of the theory becomes known and its intimate detail and qualities are explored, these peace entities will see to add their mission and numbers to the exponential growth of the culture of world peace particularly because the theory is for them and because the proof alone is certain to add vitality to existing efforts and vigor to their unique missions. After all, what part of world peace doesn't belong to our world?

14. If the general theory for a culture of world peace does turn out to be the cultural evolutionary trigger that its framework suggests it to be, then there is a great message for the religious or mystical pursuit of inner peace. As further cultural evolution means expansion into a new conscious realm, a realm where it is likely that those certainties which adorned earlier believes, will also turn out to be not only critical building blocks but part and parcel of something immensely bigger and far more wonderful than we ever dreamt before. Consider the size of the universe we knew before we discovered other galaxies and the expansion of the universe, to the majesty of a universe populated by hundreds of billions of galaxies and the anticipation

that we may finally understand the mystery of how exactly we fit in this universe and why.

15. That humanity and all other life operating within an active culture of world peace as declared here, where a realized idea of peace is an expandable and elastic instrument for the propagation of the conscious and physical duality that is objectified as PEACE. Therefore the theory predicts that, just as humanity must travel through the Anthropocene landscape, so must its conscious landscape suit the gravity of the challenges that lie ahead and balance them and itself with a measure of happiness that is afforded by the growing experience of world peace.

16. Perhaps the most unique prediction of the theory is about an effect stemming from the reconciliation of the human species with itself and the human species with the world. As life takes center stage in the human drama and the drama is about all of life in the planet, human cultural evolution in an environment of reconciliation with the world (Nature really) will tend to reset life on the original developmental path and because of the Human/Nature partnership in the making of the world, the human species is likely to evolve into a new species

(perhaps a Homo-integralis; the integral being with itself and the world) who likely be the heir of these efforts in the long run in the new world.

Is the General Theory for a Culture of World Peace just another utopian dream?

While the direct answer is emphatically NO! However, a brief explanation for why that is so can be approached this way.

The theory enters the world stage at a moment in history where the survival of humanity and of life on Earth for that matter, could also be thought of as a utopian dream. Given the obvious presence of not only CEGE but also a state of humanity where life, is constantly superseded by economic stability concerns regardless of the consequences. Therefore by that measure, a theory of world peace, which took over half a century in its formulation is most definitely not what one would call a stretch, at all.

Getting the world back up on a course parallel to life and towards a level of sustainable continuity is not going to be easy, it will demand sacrifices, and at times the odds may appear insurmountable. However we all know what the answer is, if we collectively as a species do not take the first step.

Suppose we could appraise independent of what we now know to be true, the odds for success regarding our ancestors at the beginning of the human experience. There we have, a mostly naked and naturally unarmed creature, walking upright and scampering on the plains foraging for food, cleaning carrion after the bigger and better armed predators finished their meal, these are early humans whom themselves were prey to other hunters, you know the rest of our story... What would you have thought if someone at that point in time had said to you; that creature will someday evolve to not only dominate all life in the world but will also change the make up, the chemistry, the function, the shape and the relationship of all life on Earth. Then to top it all and to his own peril, the creature will unintentionally unleash a global mass extinction event of his own making. Would you have thought that idea, to be a far-fetched utopian dream?

Humanity's resolve to triumph over CEGE is a campaign to rebuild the world we almost destroyed, our victory will reveal itself in the shape of a new world, A culture of world peace is an instrument that enables the dream but, like with all instruments, it requires a player and lots of practice, practice, practice.

The instrument is here, are you ready to play?

Tiité Baquero – Naples Florida

A supplemental word about culture

Because of the duality that exists between the domain of Nature at large and the domain of Human nature as active forces with distinct characteristics, it is sensible to consider that a single definition for a concept like culture, would not suit both of them, at least at this moment in history when their differences are on a collision course with CEGE and its mass extinction agenda for life on Earth.

While Nature's culture is something that we are just beginning to glimpse at in detail and at a depth for which we never had the conscious instruments required or the upgraded fundamental knowledge to do so. Further, convincing evidence of our cultural incompleteness brought up by the onset of the Anthropocene, reveals that a troubling gap remains between the relation of human culture and the culture of life itself.

Therefore it may suffice for now to assign culture in Nature as a measure of the distinction between its process and our interpretation of it, as it is our interpretation of Nature and us what constitutes the bulk of human culture.

As the appearance of a theory of peace is occurring at a cultural boundary between having no realized concept of peace and the appearance of one such concept, then culture may be loosely and broadly defined in reference to the closest and most relevant cultural boundaries that we can observe. I'm thinking about cultural boundaries that we have crossed or that we are about to cross which help us frame a working definition of what is meant by culture in relation to the general theory for a culture of world peace.

Map onto that, three (3) cultural boundaries that we can observe.
1. The cultural boundary between us and other primates.
2. The cultural boundary in which we live at present without peace
3. The cultural boundary in which peace enters the human equation

You will be quick to notice that cultural boundary (1.) is the province of primates who remain tied to Nature and their culture is limited to their natural state. We crossed that cultural boundary long ago but their culture can be defined as; encoded information consisting of local behavioral variations occurring at least initially for non-genetic or non-ecological ambitions but are cultural variations which persist beyond the generation of their originators. That is an instance of culture within the natural boundary.

In that framework behaviors related to the impulse of violence or tranquility can be understood as the equivalents of war and peace in human terms.

Cultural boundary (2.) occurs within the boundary of a human nature of our own making in cultural isolation from Nature, while culture can be defined similarly as in (1) our increased control of abstract ideas led us to expand the boundary far way from nature but did so at our own expense in actual practice.

In the context of boundary (2.) human culture may be described as the current sum-total of encoded information, which constitutes the diverse array of interpretative and operational notions about the world and humanity within our civilized global society.

Human culture then, may be considered as an ever growing collection of symbolic meanings that are acted-out in a myriad of ways, that are interpreted in a myriad of ways, that are understood in a myriad of ways and expressed in a myriad of ways, however all are about the way we have understood the world, our place in it and the way we live in the world.

These tendencies have been articulated through the five (5) foundational organizing agencies of civilization, which became culture's primary institutions, namely, Government, the Sciences, Religion, Industry and Media, which in their historic and current diversity have driven human culture to its present state.

As the known sum-total of human culture driving civilization has turned out to be unsustainable to itself, to life in general and to the Earth's natural resources, it can be presumed that human culture is either incomplete or it is an evolutionary dead-end.

If we accept the incomplete thesis, then appropriate additional cultural instruments must be sought and installed, with their use becoming a critical part of the response to the challenges posed by the Anthropocene epoch.

Cultural boundary (3.) is the next boundary that we may cross and for which the general theory for a culture of world peace is intended.

With the addition of a culture of world peace and the adaptive cultural instruments which support not only the structure of peace but by extension go on to upgrade the overall cultural context of humanity to better respond to the demands of the Anthropocene epoch.

Therefore human culture in the context of boundary (3.) may be defined as a compilation of

all three boundaries that are excited by a fresh
wave of cultural evolution, itself punctuated by
our reconciliation to our own kind and our own
kind with the world, to work collectively in
response to new survival challenges in what is
undoubtedly a new world.

August 24, 2014
Tiité Baquero – Naples Florida
Copyright © Tiité Baquero 2014
All rights reserved

Note:

The general theory for a culture of world peace is
an independent work of my own and therefore
lacks specific citations and references because
the bulk of the material is the result of original
ideas of my own that are based on an informal
survey of the main body of the human history of
ideas and of my own observation of Nature.

Therefore, this work is better understood in
connection with the body of formative works that
comprise my overall work on peace, which
culminates with the declaration of the general
theory.

I'm currently working on a book that
encapsulates the extent and character of my work
on peace over the last 57 years, in which many of
the ideas as stated during the many years of their

development are updated and revised as it is typical with works in progress and the revision work that they entail as the ideas are refined.

Nevertheless the ideas contained in early publications are themselves a testament to their origin and evolution as well as acceptable reference to the material that finally became a general theory for a culture of world peace.

While the archival reference is vast, some of the material reference highlighting key relevant data is published in various forms and provides, I think, adequate documentation of the general direction of my work and of what the data therein contributed to the overall initiative.

Update to note:
The Next Great Migration is the book that was mentioned in progress above. The declaration of the general theory for a culture of world peace is included in the book for obvious relevance and continuity.

The worldwide **Peace Marker Project** collective is
the flagship project, which is expected upon
completion to provide a definitive proof to the
General Theory for a culture of world peace.
It must be noted that even as a work in progress,
it already exhibits the minimum requirements
needed to fulfill the hypothesis for the general
theory for a culture of world peace.

"The Proof"

Chapter IX
The Worldwide Peace Marker collective

A theory can be a very useful guide to discovery but it is not much if it cannot be proven and all the talk in the world would not do, until something credible, substantial happens that is accountable and verifiable by all of the observers.

A general theory for a culture of world peace would have been impossible during the Holocene epoch for reasons that scholars will hopefully discuss for years to come, providing we survive, however, I will suggest that a prominent reason was that humanity's adolescence had not played itself out.

What I mean is that, the cultural context that came in to view during the 4th millennium BC that instituted civilization in the Near East with the rise of Sumer, often cited as "the cradle of civilization" and all of the gifts it bequeathed civilization, like year round farming, the potter's wheel, a writing system, central government, law, the empire, slavery, social stratification and organized warfare as well as the foundations for astronomy and mathematics and many more inventions that are still with us in the modern age.

What this tell us today and at this crucial moment in history is, that in spite of all of our so called modernity with all of its gadgets and gizmos, we are still a "Bronze Age People" and that, I propose, is the real length of our adolescence as a civilized species.

There is not, a more eloquent point in our history, in which we can look at ourselves for what we really are, than in the face of the state of the world at present. There we have a clear reflection of our innocence, to stand as witness for our human adolescence, together with the already apparent critical health of civilization, and of the entire earth's biosphere. In short, there we have inescapable evidence to the incompleteness of our human cultural context.

The Anthropocene epoch therefore is not a judgment against humanity but rather, a reality about it and it is on that reality that we should act and act quickly. As I said before the Anthropocene epoch is a big enough geological marker that we can use to signal the beginning of our adulthood as a species as well.

A general theory for a culture of world peace as we have seen previously, if proven, will provide the first of the missing components lacking in civilization and the arrival of the trigger impulse for humanity to move forward with the activity that can stabilize civilization, the global environment and hopefully stall the on going mass extinction event.

The proof itself is another matter altogether and a fairly difficult problem that also took decades to workout but happily I managed to solve it and thanks to the Data-A aesthetic I have been able to enlist art to help to provide irrevocable and substantive proof for the theory.

Not to be pretentious but for lack of a similar example, just a century ago and almost to the day as I write this chapter, Albert Einstein was hurrying to complete his field equations, which are in fact the core of Einstein's General theory of relativity, for a scheduled presentation at the Prussian Academy of Sciences on November 15, 1915.

Back then, he, as I do now a hundred years later, was concerned with the proof to his theory, both of us after evidence of something that never existed before and again both of us working on the outside of academically accepted ideas.

Einstein's proof required a solar eclipse and a number of heroes recruited from the astronomical community who were willing to photograph the event that finally proved General relativity.

Similarly, I'm recruiting art and 198 heroes from the artist community to create a planetary event that will also deliver the proof, in this case, to a general theory for a culture of world peace.

Curiously, there is an interesting detail between Einstein's work and my work and it is that his work ushered in the nuclear age and that mine may actually go on to mitigate its warfare and industrial implications; I think he would have liked to see that happen.

The planetary event is called the Worldwide Peace Marker Project collective and it is, as best as possible, a carefully constructed point-by-point application of Data-A aesthetics, its three principles and two perspectives, which I mentioned in chapter VI, plus the experience and results of previous experimental projects, all of which entered the project as critical design and criteria.

The Worldwide Peace Marker Project collective was lunched in 2002, and continues to make progress in 2015 as I write these words; now, let's take a look at the project itself.

The "Worldwide Peace marker Project collective" or "WPMP collective" for short is the flagship project for Data-A art as a global movement and the eventual proof to the general theory for a culture of world peace.

Therefore it is critical that I explain what I mean by the flagship for the Data-A movement; movement itself in the sense of a rapid progress of events. For the first three decades of development the fundamental thesis of the work involved was steered towards including life itself as part of the art process as a new source of meaning, all the while seeking to eliminate the notion of a gap between art and life and thereby establish unification between the two.

When the Data-A manifesto was published in 2012, the thesis for the movement consolidated the fact that Data-A was indeed an aesthetic exploring a greater role for life itself in assigning meaning to art. However on January of 2014, empirical evidence was obtained of the unification between art and life, providing an indication that art itself had indeed evolved and that its development was a perfect fit with the onset of the Anthropocene epoch and thus Data-A art qualifies as a movement emerging in that epochal period. Chapter X deals with the detail of that development.

The vital importance, regarding the elimination of the gap between art and life and their unification as an aesthetic of life is, that it blew open the doors for art to play a critical role in the unification of humanity to itself as a single species and for the unification prospects between humanity and the world.

Therefore WPMP collective as a flagship for Data-A art presents a project where art can rightfully operate at a global level with critical possibilities to offer such as a culture of world peace, backed up by a general theory to support its claim and a number of aesthetic first principles and perspectives to light the way.

Now, let us take a closer look at the WPMP collective first at its individual components or constituent parts and then altogether as a global work of art.

WPMP collective as an art object
WPMP collective can be described as an installation work of art, meaning that it is a work of art that has 198 component parts called Peace Markers, which are placed at specified locations in 198 separate nations around the world.

Figure1:
A Peace Marker is a sculptural stainless steel object measuring 12" inches in height; it is hollow and weights 16 pounds. It has anchoring bolts to attach it to a pedestal or other permanent public exhibition scheme.

The top surface is engraved with the legend "Peace Marker" and the name of the particular "nation" for which it was assigned. Also, the top surface has at the center an embedded "Peace Coin" (See figure 10)

Therefore, 198 Peace Markers are required for installation in 198 sovereign nations to complete the installation work of art.

The kind of art that makes WPMP collective possible comes from an art movement founded by Tiité called Data-A art which is described as an information based aesthetic, whose principal aim is to "explore a greater role for life itself in defining art's meaning."

WPMP collective as a collaborative work of art
The WPMP collective is a collaborative work of art that is formed, by recruiting 198 Artists, each, a native from each of the 198 Sovereign Nations selected. Each artist enters the collaborative as an Artist Ambassador to his/her nation of birth. The resulting Artists Ambassador collective is fundamentally grounded in a few key activities, which assure the completion of the project, although there are no limitations for their further involvement, beyond the completion of the WPMP collective.

These are:
1. The Ambassadors receive and place the Peace Marker within their respective Nation.
2. The Ambassadors participate in a pledge of "non opposition to the idea of world peace" a stand, which the "Peace Marker"

itself, represents physically as a point of peace.

3. Each ambassador would be aware that he/she and the marker that they sponsor, becomes the physical and aesthetic root and beginning of that nation's culture of peace

4. 198 Artist Ambassadors and 198 Peace Markers as a collaborative thereby, create a collective array at a global scale, which generates a true minimal working aesthetic model of what would become a culture of world peace. (More later)

WPMP collective as a global work of art
The idea of a global work of art is a hard idea to grasp, mainly, because there has never been a work of art that has been declared as such, having sufficient geographical presence in structure, substance or narrative to qualify as a global work of art.

The WPMP collective since its launch in 2002 has had to deal with that global scale perception problem. Happily ten years later, in January 2012 a group of researchers began to create an Earth-size virtual instrument called the "Event Horizon Telescope," the mission; to take a first ever, good picture of the black hole at the center of our galaxy, the Milky Way.

Mr. Sheperd Doeleman of MIT and his team want to create a network of up to 50 radio telescopes around the world, which will work in concert to get the job done. "In essence, we are making a virtual telescope with a mirror that is as big as the Earth," Doeleman said, "Each radio telescope we use can be thought of as a small silvered portion of a large mirror. With enough such silvered spots, one can start to make an image."

That dramatic development casts a bright and credible light onto the WPMP collective as their striking similarity as earth-size-objects helps to illustrate the global scale perception problem very nicely.

The Event Horizon Telescope is an instrument geared to reveal an image of the mysterious black hole; likewise WPMP collective seeks to create an instrument through which the abstract idea of "world peace" is also made visible for the first time.
The Event Horizon Telescope is made from an array of 50 radio telescopes around the world and WPMP collective is made from an array of 198 Peace Markers around the world.

The Event Horizon is in fact a virtual telescope with a mirror as big as the Earth; WPMP collective is a physical work of installation art that also encompasses the whole earth

The Event Horizon Telescope thinks of each radio telescope as a small portion of the giant mirror, where enough such points can start to make an image, WPMP collective's Peace Markers; make an array that also reveals an image of world peace that is seen through a culture of world peace.

The following images will further illustrate the global implications of WPMP collective in contrast to the previously mention scientific initiative.

The Event Horizon Telescope is aimed at revealing aspects of the universe which we have never seen before and likewise the WPMP collective is also an attempt to reveal aspects of the idea of world peace, which have never been seen before.

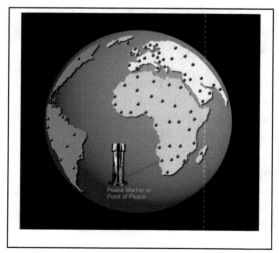

Figure 2: (previous page) Shows Peace Markers as points of peace distributed amongst the visible geographic sample of a number of nations located within this view of the Earth.

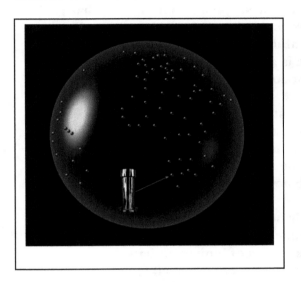

Figure 3: Shows the Earth removed, leaving behind the array of Peace Markers, which form an installation work of art that effectively corresponds to the size of planet Earth.

WPMP collaborative as a model of a culture of world peace
While a culture of war is something that is instantly recognizable in our everyday experience, so is the wide variety of ways in

which the culture of war has been expressed by the human experience throughout time; as the thousands of existing history books suggest.

However, you may be surprised to find, that, that is not the case with a culture of world peace and that one can confidently say, that an independent history of peace is absent in most human culture either ancient or current.

Clearly, if such history of peace is absent at present and one has never existed before, then, it stands to reason that peace was never a human priority or that the motivation to institute a culture of peace never really presented itself.

That is definitely not the case today, as we enter the new Anthropocene epoch, which describes a world where the effects of human activity, have turned into a formidable enemy of all life on Earth. This is an enemy so powerful that it gives origin to a new level of global warfare and that also requires a culture of world peace that is capable to help organize humanity to launch an effective attack against it.

Therefore, WPMP collective as a model of a culture of world peace is more than a work of art. It is art (Data-A art) responding to a new challenge to which we have to respond collectively and for which we need new cultural instruments to do so. Data-A art is uniquely suited to create models where such cultural instruments come into play.

By modeling a culture of world peace, the WPMP collective activates a social process beyond the boundaries of the work of art and into the realm of social science where the model can also become a proof to a general theory for a culture of world peace.

The huge advantage for WPMP collective in that social process is that art can preside over the initial conditions and set off the chain reaction which becomes the actual start-up for an active and flourishing culture of world peace.

To accomplish that, Data-A art provides the aesthetic environment where the model culture of world peace can come into existence and it does that from a point of total absence, more precisely from a "ZERO" point of existence or total nothing. That way, the culture emerges fresh and uncompromised by any previous conceptions or notions regarding the idea of peace or of a culture of world peace.

Furthermore, as the environment for an independent culture of world peace is created by the Peace Markers, the Artist Ambassadors, their collective "non" opposition to the idea of world peace, all happening in the global arena of 198 nations around the world, causing thereby the fundamental model of world peace to take hold in the real world.

It is worth mentioning, that the idea of world peace is appearing at the same time that the idea of a "global society" is also taking hold and becoming an unavoidable reality as well. The fact is, that the idea of a culture of world peace is at least 5,000 years behind the well-established culture of war as it is in our civilized global society.

Think of it as if each Peace Marker and matching Ambassador are in fact the start of a culture of peace in each selected nation and thereafter, each nation becomes a culture of peace branch giving form to what will turnout to be a global tree where the combined 198 branches could be seen as a culture of world peace tree.

In figure 4 and figure 5, I will try to illustrate how a culture of world peace enters into existence, and how compelling the initial conditions outlined by non-opposition to a culture of world peace allows the culture to emerge from nothing or a zero value.

DETAIL # 1

Figure 4: Shows a number of Peace Markers in place, with their corresponding Ambassadors in their assigned geographical locations around the world.

Detail #1: Shows how the "Zero value or non-existence of a culture of world peace" is broken to allow for the "information" chain reaction that brings a culture of world peace -into existence. (See figure 5)

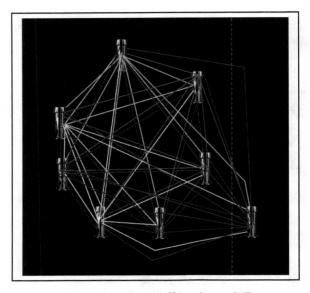

Figure 5: Shows detail #1 where 8 Peace
Markers and their Ambassadors exchange their
pledge of "non opposition" to the idea of world
peace amongst themselves, thereby generating a
network made of 56 communication lines which
start a chain reaction that extends to all 198 Peace
Markers for a total of 39,006 non opposition lines
to the idea of world peace, which in term create a
network that reveals that a culture of world peace
has been born.

I must point out that, as the network of their
narrative reaches critical mass, that is all 198
points of peace are aware of each other, the
resulting network (as seen in figure 5) creates a
network which reveals that a new culture is born

out of a global non-opposition to the existence of a culture of world peace and this constitutes a proof for the general theory.

WPMP collective as an Anthropocene instrument on behalf of all life
The Anthropocene epoch is described here for our purposes, as the name scientists have given to the current geological state of the Earth that is the result of centuries of human activity which when examined at a planetary scale, reveal; a world made by us, with characteristics that the planet never had before. Overall, the planet is steadily growing hostile to life as we know it and continuing to deteriorate by the unsustainable demands that human activity places upon the earth's environment.

While humanity is just coming to terms with the Anthropocene epoch, there is no shortage of evidence that the Anthropocene is here, that it is real and that we are all in it. At the moment I write these lines, the U.N. report by the IPCC (Intergovernmental Panel on climate change) highlights… "Yokohama, March 31, 2014 - Global warming will disrupt food supplies, slow world economic growth and may already be causing irreversible damage to nature."

Those warnings are mentioned only in connection to "climate change." The reader must also realize that climate change is but one characteristic of the Anthropocene epoch, one amongst dozens of other issues which together greatly magnify the critical nature of the threat on all life which is posed by the Anthropocene epoch.

Here is perhaps the most valuable kernel regarding the WPMP collective and surely about the framework of ideas that make Data-A art, arguably, an aesthetic movement uniquely suited for the Anthropocene epoch.

It follows that if you can accept that thus far we have managed to push the notion of peace, from the familiar purely abstract idea to a conceivable beginning point where peace's own physical and cultural presence becomes an observable global and undeniable fact. Then we can ask the next logical question...

How is the WPMP collective an Anthropocene instrument?

To approach an answer, we have to take into account the fact that the Anthropocene epoch is a lot more complex than we know, a lot more menacing than it seemed at first glance and that if anything, the Anthropocene is surely, a time of reckoning, a time for collective action and cultural growth, or a time to continue to deny its presence, to stay on the course we are on and go extinct along with most of life on earth.

WPMP collective is an Anthropocene instrument simply because it presents a model of the kind of collective effort that is necessary to confront the world we created, for which, we do not have in place, the cultural instruments needed to respond to the assault of the many calamities which are already at our door.

The Anthropocene response from humanity requires nor just an alliance of all of humanity working together as a single species, but also a culture capable of organizing, sustaining, nurturing and empowering such an alliance with the cultural instruments that are required, which by the way, are instruments which we never had before and that needed to be invented. (See chapter VI)

The WPMP collective generates a model for a "culture of world peace" that is born into the Anthropocene to become one such instrument, an instrument that allows us to view the idea of "world peace" in a way that we never saw it before. Just as Galileo Galilei's telescope allowed people in 16th century to see the moon in a way never seen before, while at the same time opening the door to astronomy and the stars for the whole of humanity.

The WPMP collective model of a culture of world peace is perhaps the most important instrument being made at this time and a critical great first step by humanity as we enter the realities of the Anthropocene epoch.

It follows that; we can now answer the question about WPMP collective as an Anthropocene instrument...
If you grant me that CEGE gives you a wider view of what is actually lurking in the environment of the Anthropocene epoch, then you may also embrace the fact that if we have done so poorly on just one issue "global warming," just what kind of a chance do we have against all of the other issues, which are just as, if not more menacing than global warming and worse yet as a combined force.

 The answer then is that, the WPMP collective models and brings into existence a culture of world peace capable of activating into action a concept of world peace where humanity and the whole of its global society can see a way to begin to work together to fight on the ultimate war, against CEGE the ultimate enemy. This time the fight is for life on Earth.
Without the unifying influence of a culture of world peace, our global society may not be able to organize a viable response against CEGE. (See chapter V)

Last but not least there is one more component of WPMP collective which deals with the economic dimensions of a culture of world peace.

Consider that, if a culture of war has derived huge economic incentives, so must a culture of world peace be able to offer similar economic incentives. I'm talking about the Peace Coin...

Figure 9: Shows that at the top of each Peace Maker, in addition to the engraving of Peace Marker and the name of the Nation to which the marker is assigned to represent in the WPMP collective. There is also embedded at the center of the top, a Peace Coin.

Figure 10: shows a Peace Coin, which is the first ever, currency, minted specifically to foster a culture of world peace.

The Peace Coin is physically and conceptually embedded in the model of a culture of world peace as the economic seed from which world peace will develop its unique cultural economic structure from which the culture will in term derive the incentives and rewards which may be part of the global economic structure, which characterizes civilization's passage through the Anthropocene epoch.

Even though the embedded Peace Coin atop the Peace Marker is made from pure sterling silver, its value as a currency enters at "Zero," so that the Peace Coin too, enters the project in non-opposition to the idea of an economic incentive that is built within an emerging culture of world peace.

As the WPMP collective nears its completion or soon after, participating nations may be persuaded to celebrate the project's lofty goals and cultural opportunities and decide to mint a Peace Coin of their own, with an assigned value to circulate within their economy. Those Peace Coins in circulation will retain the original design as shown here but utilize the other side of the coin for national identity and the assigned value of the currency.

One can only marvel at the potential results stemming from the introduction of real value to a currency of world peace to empower a culture of world peace to do what no other cultural direction may be able accomplish, particularly in regards to the recovery of the spirit of human civilization and its ability to restore the Earth to remain a sustainable cradle for all life.

Finally, permit me to loosely assemble all that we have read into a simple glance at what the after effect of the WPMP collective leaves behind once the project is completed.

Is WPMP collective a template for cultural evolution?

The design behind the construction of a model for a culture of world peace was no easy task as the design required components which were perhaps within our reach but that had never been fitted into instruments to be added to our human cultural tool kit, that is to say that their structure and use, is seen for the first time in the design of the WPMP collective and brought up as critical components of the general theory for a culture of world peace.

Without going deep into the reasons why we never really discovered the "instruments" that I discussed in chapter VI it may suffice to say that, one; the need to develop them never arose before in the history of humanity and two; their use is a development that coincides with the onset of the Anthropocene epoch, which is the place where such instruments are suitable for use on behalf of all life on Earth.

The first thing to point out is that the WPMP collective is a work where art and life are fully reconciled which is why the model it is producing works just as well in the gallery or museum as it does in the real world. Data-A art is an aesthetic of reconciliation between art and life unified as two compatible flows of information; and that is the subject of the next chapter.

"Cognitive Escape"

Chapter X
Data-A and Cultural evolution

This chapter should really be the subject of an entire book and I hope that I live to see the subject treated by more able hands in depth and that future generations benefit from the seminal ideas that are presented here with such economy and necessary brevity.

It is a catastrophe, that at a time when reading is dramatically vital, humanity seems to not want to be bothered with anything larger, than the allotment of words that fit within the precious few seconds of the average attention span, or the aversion that we seem to have developed for reading material that has substance and meaning, beyond the usual diet of kitschy and banal commentary that populates most media.

There is a built in benefit in all of it however, one that I mentioned before and that is a reliable cultural benchmark that clearly separates the human cultural high point at the end of the Holocene and the new prospects for cultural evolution in the Anthropocene.

Cultural evolution is a difficult and contentious issue not only academically but throughout the entire spectrum and history of human society, not for the absence of great contributing work for its understanding, but because culture itself is so stratified and bent conveniently to suit a large number of narrow objectives, having to do more with ideology and the hegemony of the human species over all other life, than they do with the actual process of cultural evolution, as a unique whole-life-on-Earth phenomenon.

In the Anthropocene epoch, that reality is surfacing with great clarity, as all of life on earth is being challenged, by the effects of human activity upon the natural process, a process to which we and all other life are an inextricable part of.

That connection between us and all other life is a connection that has been missing and that we have to restore before we can understand our cultural evolution and how that understanding is vital to the reorganization of our survival strategy in the Anthropocene epoch.

What became Data-A art was the result of a pursuit, to find a way to reconnect human nature and Nature at large, a lofty goal that was ignored and ridiculed for the first 30 years, but as we will see, was not only realized in the most marvelous of ways, but also gave us a new view into the puzzle of cultural evolution and more importantly, a survival clue as to how we may use our reconnection with nature to stabilize life on earth.

The story goes that after work I had initiated in 1983 with the installation of a work called "Homage to the Orange River Valley," (see image below) in Lee County Florida and at the mouth of the Orange River and the Caloosahatchee River and within a nature preserve frequented by the endangered West Indian Manatee, whose silhouetted images are depicted by the sculpture. The intimate story of this piece is intriguing to say the least but too long to tell for our purpose here, it will suffice to say that it is one of the foundations upon which Data-A aesthetic was built.

This work was to become the centerpiece of a larger installation called Earth Gallery one 1990, an ambitious work attempting to encompass a presence within the 428 square miles of Lee -

county's coastal waters, to provide the backdrop for a single work of art that could initiate the dialog about the reconciliation between art and life or ostensibly between human nature and Nature at large; hence the title "Earth Gallery One" or, you could also say, exhibit "A" for a new aesthetic concept with global implications.

The work is composed of a total of 12 Sentries, (see figure11) 10 of which are in a six square mile cluster that is known as the Mills Manatee Mile along the shores of Galt Island near Saint James city, There is 1 at the Punta Rassa boat ramp and 1 at Stero Bay, near Fish Tale canal and Coon key Island. The latter one, being the one we will focus on as the brief of this chapter.

A sentry in this project was created to do exactly what the word sentry describes, that is, a guard stationed at a location to stand watch, except that this time, a scale down version of the sculptural silhouette of two manatees as presented by the Homage to the Orange River Valley centerpiece on the Caloosahatchee river.

As all of the twelve sentries had posts or positions of duty, in fairly busy navigable waters and would be seen by many people over the years, it was only proper that they also be given specific names representing a particular institution of civilization and legends to announce the particular pledges, all of which, go along with the idea of a culture working together with Nature to the benefit of all life.

Figure 11: showing the Friendship Sentry

"The basis of environmental recovery lay in oneness with creation and with ourselves – enjoy it"

Figure 12: showing Friendship Sentry in 1990

"The recovery of Earth is a task accomplished by Man and nature in mutual friendship – let's do it"

Twenty five years ago, this project was as invisible in its meaning and cultural significance as the needs for environmental recovery of the world's ocean and creatures like the West Indian Manatee are today.

In 2013, Florida lost 16% of the estimated total manatee population, while the recovery of the West Indian manatee is a fairly popular initiative the actual progress over the last quarter of a century has very little to show for, with regards to direct veterinary preventive medicine or effective measures for conservation of their food resources or on the quality of their ambient water.

People boating by the work all these years saw signs, not sculptures, this is mostly because art had never been placed in the context of life, out there in Nature and away from museums, galleries and the heavily monetized art market. This was art placed to be directly in contact with the public and Nature with no other purpose than to educate people and to serve the Human/Nature initiative.

There has always been a gap between us and the world, which kept the idea of man versus Nature or of humanity as separate from Nature alive, thereby, perpetuating the "us versus the world " a culture of separateness that was also perceived by the arts as the gap between art and life.

Famously, it was the gap between art and life that Robert Rauschenberg spoke about or more clearly the gap between humanity and Nature at large.

I had been working on that problem since 1980 and had proposed that art would have to focus on "life" and thereby evolve to be inclusive of "life itself," meaning, that the whole of natural activity which comprises life on Earth, would have to play a greater role in assigning meaning to art.

That is basically the thesis behind Data-A art; however, the trouble was that to close the gap, the evidence would have to show in no uncertain terms that Nature would have to manifest itself onto the work of art, independently from the artist, but somehow jointly to create between the two an eloquent and verifiable single work of art.

The proof to that thesis would take 25 years to come along but it did. In January 14, 2014 a pair of Osprey eagles was found to be nesting atop of the friendship sentry and there was evidence that the nest had newly hatched young.

Now, that occurrence could be attributed to a whole variety of circumstances from a miraculous intervention to just a fluke or a chance happening, but the fact that it occurred on a sentry whose legends as written, waited for a quarter of a century for their fulfillment with - Nature is a most remarkable occurrence that only needed to happen once to validate the thesis and it did.

Figure13: showing the Osprey pair nesting atop of the Friendship Sentry

We humanity are one of those remarkable natural occurrences that can also be called a fluke of a chance happening as nothing like us has ever appeared before or since in the history of life on Earth; but it did.

Figure 14: the proof of the Data-A thesis and the birth of new art and life unification paradigm

The gap between art and life has been irrevocably closed and the doors for reconciliation between humanity and the world where opened.

With that groundbreaking moment, modern art set foot on the Anthropocene epoch and humanity has an art whose meaning is also informed and derived from life itself.

As I write this chapter, the Osprey has had two successful nesting seasons and the collaborative work has produced four offspring eagles as further evidence of Art's new relationship with life.

There is however, another powerful message, which clarifies most of what I have been saying in the previous chapters, regarding a culture of peace and about the tenacity of suggesting a general theory for a culture of world peace, where of all things, art is the one shouldering the burden of the proof. Furthermore, a project like the WPMP collective, being capable of delivering to humanity a condition of peace, which it does, provides us with a kind of peace culture that has only existed in prayers and in the imagination of people for thousands of years.

The message therefore, is about Cultural evolution and the fact that the elimination of the art and life duality or of the proverbial gap to a single sameness, the ushering of a reconciliatory process between humanity and the world. With all of these happenings occurring amidst the survival pressures of a new Geological epoch in which the conservation of all life is to become the ultimate measure of our humanity, is almost too good to be true; happily it is.

Still, these are the unmistakable signs that cultural evolutionary triggers have been activated and that an aesthetic like Data-A, is indeed providing the cultural instruments that can get us on the way, not just to recovery, but on to the migration route to our next stage of development; our adulthood as a species.

Our notions of cultural evolution will mature under the light of our reconciliation with Nature simply because in the end we are and always will be decedents of a common ancestor to all life on earth and cultural evolution began there. It is inextricably embedded in primitive behavioral cognitive structures, which we amplified only for our own convenience in an independent move to interpret the world in our own separate way.

That was a strategy that, we know now, to have backfired because in our haste to conquer the world and each other, we forgot that our own survival was tied to the survival of all other life and that cultural evolution is tied to life and that that is the lesson we are about to learn in the classroom we built for ourselves called the Anthropocene epoch.

Behold then, how one pair of Osprey shows us the magnificence of their art, building without hands an impressive structure that we are still challenged to be able to build ourselves and of such magnificence that is suitable to bring life into the world and of such economy of material that no glue or power equipment was used nor did it produced waste or required inspection for its sufficiency as a structure.

Nature still has a lot to reveal to us as its culture is a culture of life and its idea of life is one of continuity for those creatures that manage to learn to live within its global biosphere. Cultural evolution has now placed our species where we always wanted to be at the top, now we are about learn about the responsibilities that come along with that position.

Note:
"Homage to the Orange River Valley" (page 198) is a sculptural work of art that I dedicated to Dr. Jesse R. White, a pioneer of marine mammal veterinary medicine particularly with the West Indian Manatee. He was a great mentor, teacher and friend whose guidance contributed to make this work possible.

"Conscious Migration"

Chapter XI
The next great migration

To my mind, this may be the appropriate time to bring back up the central idea of this book, which is the migration initiative. I do so because by now you may have mixed feelings about whether or not we may be able to get out of the predicament we are in or even if it is worth the trouble to try and see what can be done.

I'm an optimist-realist of sorts and I have to be, as an optimist I have done little else over the past half a century but to work on this problem, unfunded, marginalized, unappreciated, ignored by the arts and science community and saved by a handful of people whom respected my stubbornness and dedication at all cost, to a mission that hardly anybody understood or thought it was worthwhile. As a realist the price I've paid for this quest did not come as a surprise, which is why everything I have done is paid-for and it is mine to give to you to the rest of humanity and to every other creature that surely will never know where the gift comes from.

I firmly believe that we as a species have enough time to get going and that the migration initiative is as valid for hope, as denial and despair that nothing can be done is for giving up or doing nothing about it.

If the idea of migration means to move from one place to another, then, open your eyes because quite dramatically the evidence shows that we are already physically living in a new world even if we do not acknowledge or have realized that fact.

The Anthropocene epoch may be just a geological designation that we may or may not accept, but the physical conditions that prompted the need for the new geological designation are here. They have been here, by one account since July 16, 1945 and by other accounts for about 200 years or more, either way, many of us where in fact born in the Anthropocene epoch and the world of the Holocene is simply just not our world anymore.

The migration initiative comes into play as we realize that we are in a new Anthropocene world where the culture from the Holocene world, would only hasten or guarantee our extinction and that of all other life, besides, for the look of things, moving towards a new state of culture is the only alternative we have left.

Just remember that humanity was in a similar survival predicament in Africa before their eventual migration out of the continent some 60,000 years ago, scarcity of food, water and other environmental deficiencies made a migration initiative a viable alternative to the possibility of extinction.

The next great migration therefore is fundamentally a cultural migration initiative where the entire human species begins to modify its cultural context in a way that its cultural activity migrates from a self-serving, all-consuming, possession of the world, to a new role as the custodian species for life on earth.

Those look like very big shoes right now and they are, this is a long migration and not an easy one at all. On the way, we have to halt the ongoing extinction event on its tracks, repair civilization and begin a several hundred years clean up of the planet.

On the plus side, we will not go extinct and that prospect suggests, that many of the dreams about peace, freedom and the pursuit of happiness stand a chance of becoming sustainable working features of the improved human cultural context.

At the moment however, let's keep our feet on the present and take a look at what it is meant by "human cultural context" and then we will take a look at what we may need to pack-up before setting off.

The concept of a Human cultural context, I believe, is advanced here for the first time and while it is not my invention, it is an obvious result coming from the data affirming our genetic descent and the reality that we, humanity, are indeed members of the same species and as the evidence shows have consistently shared our cultural developments throughout our entire history even though their practice varies from group to group and state of civilization.

It follows that for most of our analytical history, particularly in the fields of anthropology and sociology, the concept of cultural context, has been considered as a unique feature of individual groups and their expression, as unique practices by members of a particular geographical region, national identity, social, political, spiritual persuasion and on the character of their arts, architecture and applied sciences.

The concept of a human cultural context is an Anthropocene proposition that is sponsored by a critical perspective view of humanity as a whole during its Holocene history.

It includes all of the known aspects of pre-civilization and post-civilization life, it is the compilation of all of the ideas for which a meaning has been assigned, it embraces the utility and shortcomings derived from the understanding of such ideas and beliefs, all of which provides, the framework for the survival strategy that we adopted and that is largely based upon language, values, customs and norms.

In short, the thesis of a human cultural context manifests itself as a compendium of ideas that arguably may be the overall result of the conscious development of the human species accumulated over millions of years.

What is of vital importance here is the notion that a view to a human cultural context is critical to a species whose collective effort at a global scale, is essential to finding a survival strategy away from extinction and for the continuation of life, in an Anthropocene environment that does not offer any other alternative.

It is worth noticing that when cultural differences are viewed from a critical perspective, they reveal that we are essentially the same even if the means to express them has developed significantly in their application. By way of illustration, human hostility two hundred thousand years ago involved the throwing of rocks with the intent to harm or to kill, today human hostility throws a bullet through a gun with the same intent as derived from a common root cultural context.

Taken as a whole, the cultural context of our species has been a work in progress for millions of years. It must be noted that every single word carries essentially the same meaning in every language even if the language is believed to have developed independently.

That means that the dictionaries of all of the languages relate to the same meaning and curiously, their combined lexicon adds up to what can only be called the cultural context of the human species.

To wrap up, human cultural context may be loosely defines as:

"The totality of human thought or the sum total of ideas unique to the species, their meaning, their interpretation, usage and practice all of which comprises the phenomenon of human consciousness."

Therefore, it is not to soon to suggest that it was the content of our cultural context, which guided us and our activity here to this moment in time, to this new world of the Anthropocene epoch, to our new home, to its irascible environment and to the realization that to make our way in this new world we must migrate from our Holocene cultural context to a new version of it, that can service us, civilization and provide us with a chance to a survival strategy that is favorable to all life on earth.

Nor is it too soon, to accept the reality that the essential key to most of the solutions to Anthropocene problems is culture. The limited success of most national and international environmental agreements, which now number in the hundreds, is due to the absence of the culture that would support the measures.

We could have summits and accords until the end of time and not be able to generate a culture that will embrace the measures discussed, so long as the current culture that makes the demands for the goods and services remains the same. Why?

The answer again is that a culture that lacks the cultural instruments needed to embrace the improvements is a culture doomed to repeat the precepts of the culture itself.

Therefore, the Holocene human cultural context is such a formidable problem that without real improvements to the culture itself, the sad but unavoidable future is collapse followed by extinction.

It was the magnitude of the cultural problem coupled with the magnitude of the environmental problem in light of the prospects just mentioned that prompted the idea of the cultural migration initiative. It was its familiarity to the history of so many historic, recent and ongoing human migrations and those of many other species, which gave the notion footing, as a rational alternative with ample cultural implications.

More so, since the cultural instruments provided by Data-A aesthetics, that is, its three principles plus the two perspectives, which do indeed work even as primitive and unrefined as they may seem at the onset of their service to human culture.

We may recall that most of the worthy ideas in history where proposed by people, who like me, took interest in one problem and stayed with it until it was solved or at least pushed to the next level.

The migration initiative is a wonderful and practical notion because is rooted in our own history and because each time it gave us a destination, a destination that requires resolution, effort, patience, endurance, collectivity, hope and the strength to overcome the hardships and vicissitudes that await us on the way.

Just knowing that the human project is in route to an improved cultural destination is sufficient to create a climate of confidence or even of a guarded optimism, something that the current uncertainty about the future could not possibly offer.

There is another aspect in the migration initiative that is as unprecedented as it is marvelous in so many respects and that is, that unlike any previous migrations undertaken by our species, over incredible tracks of time, many of them caused by environmental changes, certainly a great many because of war and so on, but never like this time as we have a chance to migrate in partnership with Nature itself, in a mutual alliance with the world.

When you take a moment to think about the immensity of that relationship, it will be difficult to miss the fact that this time our migration's partner is life itself.

I always found it difficult to think that our species would made it this far and accomplish so much just to fade away into extinction leaving most of our dreams and aspirations unfulfilled.

While the unification of art and life is now a fact that has an eloquent precedent to affirm its existence, it is also an occurrence that comes with a powerful message about our partnership with nature and about Nature as a migration partner with the same destination, namely, a stable environment where life as we know it may continue to evolve and flourish.
This is the point where the migration initiative becomes an interesting notion that is nicely anchored in the reality of the world.

The unification of art and life as dramatized by the Friendship Sentry in the Earth Gallery One project, is much more than a pair of Osprey nesting atop a sculpture of a pair of Manatees in the open air, who are also perched atop a pair of wooden piles, driven into the soil to secure the duality of earth and water and thereby assemble a human made structure that embraces the fundamental structure of life, a structure, which the artist embraces in the very human spirit of friendship that is declared in a pair of written pledges about how that friendship may proceed from now on.

That may not be what we see at first glance, but it is the substance of what makes the work the first true glimpse into our capacity to reconcile with the world and of our opportunity to tap Nature for the wisdom that we missed during our adolescence as a species and to partner with the process that made us who we are, to move forward and migrate to where we have never been; in harmony with ourselves and the world.

Our Anthropocene partnership between humanity and Nature then, begins in friendship and our migration spirit is thereby a collective effort of all life for the preservation of life itself. What a contrast between that and the terms of engagement during the Holocene when it was strictly us versus nature when it was destroy and conquer, when life was the least of our concerns and when we killed each other for the possession of a world that was already ours.

Can't you see that right there, in that auspicious contrast we see the start of our conscious migration, the marvelous first hint at the power of our collective effort as a single species and of the magnificence of the terms of engagement with which to enter our journey into a world that cannot be rehabilitated without our ingenuity and creativity and without the ancient wisdom of a process that gave us a mind whose cultural context now turns its sights to life.

It is also at this point when you may ask the question: How are we going to overcome the ocean of issues and cultural barriers that separate humanity into a multitude of factions and a diversified species perpetually at odds with each other into a collective that can peacefully migrate culturally?

The answer is simple; given the present odds, we will come into a collective that can peacefully migrate culturally towards our new common destination. Getting there is not easy but nothing is.

One has to be very naïve not to see that the state of humanity is riddled with hate, corruption, inequality, crime, violence, war, and the distinguishing feature of our species; our inhumanity to our own kind and our blatant disregard for life.

But those are conditions and conditions can vary and change according to given circumstances within and without our control. There is no written contract that estate that we have to behave like that in perpetuity, nor there is one to prevent us from moving away from that culture.

In spite of all of the ugly that we have learned to harvest we are still a beautiful species capable of great good, besides all that we are doing is getting together to protect life and to collectively fight our biggest war ever against the forces of CEGE in its bid to take life away from us.

Conditions are fast changing in our world and as far as I can tell there is not at this time, a plan or a set of ideas as to how to proceed forward outside of this migration initiative and the cultural tools presented here to mitigate our passage.

If I can draw an analogy between the tragedy of the RMS Titanic in 1912 and the current circumstances of the tragedy that awaits us onboard spaceship Earth, is that we have already ran into the iceberg CEGE and while the time scale is different we are already castaways in some sense, even if there are millions of people still rearranging the chairs on the first class deck, and the captains, first officers and crew have not yet decided to tell the passengers the bad news and what to do, nor are we sufficiently equipped to evacuate all of the passengers or even have a place to take them. Sadly, for Earth there is no RMS Carpathia to rescue survivors.

Happily, there is time to react and this migration initiative is a positive first step even if only as a mere suggestion with substance direction and hope of realization.

The Worldwide Peace Marker Project is the Avatar that can intervene in this chaotic and irrational moment in history to unleash a culture of world peace, whose powerful unifying force can actually rally the collective spirit of humanity to join Nature in the battle for life on Earth and win.

Peace is the only missing and unexplored dimension of human culture whose emergence at this time will serve as the glue to hold the species together, the species glued on to nature and both glued onto the world.

An improved cultural context upgrades lesser impulses and nullifies old tendencies.

The next great migration then, is a peaceful journey where humanity and nature at large will do battle with CEGE for the big prize, life itself.

Next we will take a look at what we may need to pack-up before setting sails in the new world.

"Open Reality"

Chapter XII
Setting the sails of a new reality

Up until now I have kept the narrative of this book close to the ideas being shared from an Anthropocene perspective but away from the clash of realities that is inevitable when a culture reaches its zenith and new cultural improvements move the former culture up a notch.

It is there, at that junction where human culture has always run into problems with people at odds, about what to make of it or how to react to new ideas. History is replete with these altercations, which have cost people their lives, their reputation, in some instances even war has been declared over ideas sacrificing countless lives and resources onto those altars of contention.

Furthermore, time, large tracks of time, have been sacrificed in futile efforts to stop the inevitable outcome of better ideas that explain better the reality of a particular point in our development as a species.

Similarly, what is being proposed in this book, will also, not scape the rigors of that ancient human tradition, this time however, a whole geological epoch separate my would be critics and I can only hope that their criticism be constructive and for the enhancement of the ideas, otherwise their objections would have to be backed up with better proposals and more enlightened ideas, if not, I fear that their appraisals would fall short from contributing to finding a way out of what is already a real crisis with no other solutions in sight.

Anyway, the Holocene epoch concluded with many unresolved questions and very little agreement on their fundamental nature. Prominent among them is "reality," an idea with perhaps several billion versions and not one definition powerful enough to embrace them all. Why is that?

Well, the first thing to say is that reality is a human idea and it is an idea that has been defined in many ways over the course of human history but ultimately defined within the boundaries of our cultural context in isolation to any other sources of information that may open up into a wider perception of what reality may be in a larger context.

To say that reality is the state or quality of being real, as reality is commonly defined is to go in circles, besides real compared to what? Perhaps compared to something that is just apparent? Well, that does no good either because there is a reality in being apparent.

I do not wish to begin a big discussion here on the concept of reality but I do want to point out that reality is a big unresolved Holocene idea, but one that will play a crucial role in finding our way, in the Anthropocene epoch.

I would be remised however, for not advancing at least a comment on why reality is an unresolved cultural issue. It will suffice to say that it is because, of the static quality of the human cultural context or put another way, by the tendency of the culture to assign fixed meaning to ideas in an ever-changing world, or better yet, in an ever-expanding universe.

Let's remember that not quite a century ago, the universe was this static unchanging cosmos in the human mind, until Albert Einstein and the astronomer Edwin Hubble in particular replaced that idea of the universe with an expanding and boundless object containing more galaxies than we can imagine. Thus the word "universe" was liberated from its static state to the dynamic object we are exploring today.

Reality is like that too, and we would do well by thinking of reality as a variable event, which has to be understood within that ever-changing character of fact-things, ideas in this world where time affects their day-to-day existence.

It follows that, what I suggest in this chapter with the title "setting the sails of a new reality" is that the rather static reality that brought us here, to this new set of circumstances where civilization and the environment are so significantly different, is a reality that is no longer relevant. Therefore the concept of reality that observes such circumstances and such conditions must also be different, so different in fact as to constitute a new reality.

Now, since the state of the world at present is evidence, that our human reality as it is, turned out to be insufficient, then the reality that emanates from our partnership with Nature will not only enhance our reality but also engender a sense of reality beyond anything that we can imagine as we set sails towards that understanding.

But what do I mean by a new reality?

Well, the reason that is an important question is because "new" is a key word to understanding what is meant by a new reality. New, is a word that we associate with "appearing for the first time" as if whatever-new-refers to had never existed and that was fine to describe a lot of our inventions and discoveries. However "new" in partnership with Nature, adds on to the word a fresh layer of meaning because in Nature, new, is really a fresh look for an old recipe with modifications.

Therefore when I speak of a new reality in the context of our Anthropocene world, I'm saying that our Holocene cultural context is being freshen up by our partnership with Nature to have a new look with modifications without losing any of the original meaning.

If we had by chance understood the idea of new in this fashion before, we would have saved ourselves all of the trouble we've had and still have with the word evolution.

The reason Nature has never produced any garbage has a lot to do with nature's penchant for sustainable continuity and for the way that sufficiency allows for materials to be passed around from the top of the life-web to the bottom and back again in continuity without waste. Think about that one for a minute will you!

It follows, that our Holocene cultural context is vital to the new reality in the Anthropocene, as it represents the original building blocks upon which Nature's influence will help us craft what I mean as a new reality.

I've mentioned Nature in this book almost as much as the word Anthropocene, however the need to do so is justified by the fact that we are focusing on life here and while nature is the vessel where all life resides the Anthropocene is the environment where all life is at stake.

But, Nature is another key word and when we define it as the material world, especially as surrounding humankind and existing independently of human activities, we run smack into the reason why we are so far in the ditch, we have made up an idea that has kept us outside of the very miracle that produced us and that we nearly destroyed.

Nature, as we are discovering at the beginning of our adulthood as a species, is much, much more than that. By way of illustration, we are like the kid who discovers how much work is really involved in raising a child, after years of having taken her own mother's work for granted.

Nature is the substance and the animated material from which all that there is and all that will ever be finds its origin and from where everything forges its own path into existence and where everything exists in conformity with all of the other paths of existence.

Now, nature no longer looks like the shabby partner suggested by the Holocene definition of nature AH!

Nature is not just the ideal partner but also the only partner we can have that is a real specialist at life, while Nature may not have all of the answers it does have, all of the ones that Nature has found so far in the last 13.798 billion years.

In setting the sails of a new reality in partnership with the reality master, Nature, human culture is bound to evolve from the independent culture of one species to the collective culture of one Earth and may be, to the multiform culture of one universe.

We are thereby setting our sails high and why not; we need to catch the fast winds of creativity and imagination and allow them to fill our sails.

I mentioned briefly that a new reality did not meant the loss of already gained meaning and of the words we have assigned to carry said meaning, on the contrary we must pack up all of our Holocene knowledge because as we have seen first hand in this chapter how the static meaning of one single word can be unpacked into so much more substance, meaning and associative value to the whole of culture, that it would be unthinkable to leave behind anything we may be able to use to reconstruct our world.

Besides the new reality is constructed as we've seen word-by-word and idea-by-idea as the new cultural instruments and perspectives touch them as if with a magic wand to release their still hidden vitality and relationship to life.

We have to remember that at the end of the day everything, words, ideas, ideologies, concepts, the people who think them and the paper where they are printed and the world where they are found, is all information.

This universe is all about information and what we are doing in setting our sails is to begin to navigate towards becoming a part of the same universal stream of information, beginning here on Earth by rejoining Nature in partnership and using the power of our intellect to begin to repair spaceship Earth, stabilize the biosphere and move forwards to do the tasks that come, with having conquered the world and that is, to take on the proper stewardship of all life on Earth.

You may be thinking that all of this is fine as far as it goes, but what about all of the cultural differences and the rifts between ideologies and the perpetual warring amongst us, the constant streak of violence that underlies most of human culture. How are we going to keep all of that history and still move forward into a new reality?

The answer is; that from a purely Holocene human perspective it would be a monumental waste of time to take a dedicated barbarian and as if by magic transform him into a docile and life loving Jane (Jainism is a religious path of non-violence towards all living things) Furthermore, our history also contains wonderful ideas and a beautiful other side to that same coin that somehow completes our character as a species capable of great horror and also of incredible acts of compassion.

From an Anthropocene perspective however, those concerns take on a different character as the general idea is not to change humanity but rather to set it on a cultural evolutionary path with an added cultural tool kit that helps to clarify the cultural value of ideas, their net worth and how their contribution to culture is adapted, to the new reality of the epoch and to our new focus on life.

We have to keep in mind that our species may be guilty of innocence and cultural incompleteness, but those are not crimes, they are just features of our human adolescence. Consider that what we do with our own children at the end of their adolescence is not to prosecute them for those acts, but instead, we send them to school for their higher education. Similarly, what we are trying to do here is the same thing but with an entire species and this book is a dialog about some of the curriculum regarding our species' higher education.

So, what would be the outstanding difference between our current perception of reality and the new reality?

Well, now we are at the crux of this dialog because the outstanding difference is in

perception itself, in the amplification or our
perception as sentient beings no longer residing
in the isolation of our own make believe world,
but rather as part and parcel of the whole world.

Again, perception is a word addressing the
faculty of apprehending or grasping external
stimulus through the senses for processing by the
brain, so that the mind can identify and
recognize the source, thereby enabling insight
and discernment regarding the character and
quality of what is being perceived.

However, it is still much more than that when
perception itself is amplified by the influence of
new cognitive material or processing tools, as the
ones being introduced here. I could not suggest
that those new cultural instruments complete our
cultural context but I can propose that they do
constitute an upgrade which is being referred
here as a new reality.

To put that in another way, when our perception
of the world is interpreted only by our idea of the
world, we get a reality like the one we have now,
creating the kind of world we are in at the
moment.

When our perception of the world is tempered by
Nature's reality of the world, we begin to
perceive a reality that is more attuned to the
world. As the cultural instruments mentioned in

this book are extracts from nature and not my invention, they stand a chance to generate an upgrade to our perception of the world and that perception would constitute the basis of a new reality.

That reality is not only different but unlike anything we have ever experienced and that is because it is a reality sponsored by an "integral consciousness." What that means is that our perception of the world can occur in unison with the perception of all other life on Earth.

Therefore, Sufficiency – Sustainable Continuity – Integral consciousness plus Critical Perspective against the ample background of the Green Path perspective are just new tools, but also they are tools that lay at the foundations of the new reality In the Anthropocene.

In closing this chapter I'm going to anticipate an important question that I know it is best answered here.

What about God?
First of all, let us be clear to the fact that "God" is a word too and that the meaning (s) we have bestowed onto the word, not only transcend written human history to the earliest of our ancestors and into corners that we have not as yet dared to look into.

God is, to be sure, an insatiable impulse that we have taken by trial and error to great depth and to extremes somewhat irreconcilable by reason. Still, the insistence has to have some basis written in the history of existence in this universe, and it does.

At the height of Holocene culture, science has been quite severe with the narrative of God although perhaps not as severe as some devotees of God have been on one another and on devotees of other narratives of God.

On the one hand, science staunchly demands proof of God's existence on the other hand; religion vehemently offers faith as the path to an undeclared proof. Curiously, neither can offer clarity on the impulse nor can their arguments find a firm and common ground with expressed respect for life itself, nor are they cognizant of life as the original sponsor of the impulse for science and God.

In the Anthropocene epoch however, the unfolding new reality can actually offer an emolument to both camps for their labors and a surprising truce to the intolerance of their innocence, in the way of a proof to suit both arguments.

Just over a hundred years ago in 1905 Albert Einstein peeked into the proof but took only what he could carry of the process and his understanding of the ambivalence between matter, energy and light, famously expressed in his $E = mc^2$. Although it was not until several years later in 1927 that Georges Lemaitre noted that an expanding universe might be traced back to a single point of origin. Then in 1970 Stephen Hawking, George F.R. Ellis and Roger Penrose made calculations showing that time and space had a finite beginning that corresponded to the beginning of matter and energy.

What all of that means is that to the best of our knowledge matter and energy are not only the same thing but that light is the life force of the universe and since it all started there in the big bang, so did life itself.

Therefore light is life and life is light, it would seem that all that the universe has ever done is to see how many different kinds of stars can there be to radiate life. Life on earth is another kind of light driven life to which we are stars made out of stardust from that same beginning.

Therefore if science wants to understand life then that is a good place to connect what data we have thus far and if religion is also interested in finding God then religion would do well, following the light back to God's birth and trace in the history of the universe's life, the still untapped magnificence of the light-god-life-unity and the amazing things that science and mysticism can still contribute to life on Earth.

In setting up our sails to navigate through the rigors of this new Anthropocene world, a new reality is not just a good idea; it is I fear, the last good idea before the storm.

"In the Age of Life"

Chapter XIII
War in the age of life

War is to human civilization what feathers are to
a bird, we just can do without it and that is our
oldest truth. In the ancient past five great
civilizations emerged independently of each
other in Iraq, Egypt, India, China and the
Americas and all of them grew around war.

Ever since, war has been the chief driver of
culture with a permanent presence in every
human activity from cradle to death. Our
dependence on war is so great; that the whole of
human civilization would crumble without war,
while because of it and the prospects of nuclear
warfare, human civilization is also always just a
button away from total annihilation.

In this chapter, oddly enough, I'm not only going
to endorse war, but also to be a most fervent
proponent of war. I'm going to favor the longest,
the most expensive and the most profitable war
in the history of all wars combined and yet no
city will be bombed or invaded because of it.

The spoils of this war will be cultural and will
remain where they belong and victories will be
celebrated by all of humanity and human
casualties as sad as their prospect can be
imagined in war, would probably not be more

than a point of a percent of all of the casualties of war in the history of human violence. What?

Yes-dear reader, if you have taken an interest in what I've been saying, the last paragraphs will make more sense once we take a closer look at the reasons for those affirmations that I've just made about war.

In the last chapter, I declared the frequent use of the words Anthropocene and Holocene throughout the text, the trouble is that it cannot be helped as this book is happening at the junction of those two geological epochs and that I honestly think that the proper names will help us to embrace the fact that we are living in a different world.

There is however, an aspect to the Anthropocene that is perhaps more telling of our general aim and desire to survive in this new world, in spite of the critical challenges we have to face at the beginning of our cultural migration. It is an aspect that has to do with the heavy loss of plant and animal diversity that CEGE is causing at the front wave of its mass extinction campaign, that is coupled with the invasion of some of its agents into our own bodies via the food sources, water and atmospheric dispersion.

The heavy loss toll of creatures that are critical to the upkeep of the biosphere and us alive is rising daily and CEGE's hold is getting stronger, so that saying that all life is at stake is not an exaggeration by far.

So I'll like to think of the Anthropocene as the "age of life" and that is why this chapter is titled War in the age of Life. Further, I wish to show you, that what at first sight looks like a laughable contradiction, may actually turn out to be the saving grace for one of the things that we do best and that we have done the most of, for the longest of time; war.

As history shows, until now we have exclusively been fighting each other and for a variety of reasons that on close inspection are still a reenactment of an even older survival impulse, to claim a resource for one's own exclusive needs through the use of threats or violent force, an impulse that is typical to basically all of life on earth.

Fortunately, sufficiency regulates that impulse, for the most part, on most other life on earth; however, our species also amplified another primitive impulse "greed." Its pursuit nurtured in our species the addiction to power that has made us the most violent creature ever to inhabit the earth.

I propose that in the Anthropocene epoch, that in the age of life, we not only tap on that evolutionary accomplishment, but also that we take it to a new all time level of efficiency, this time against our first real "other" CEGE, an enemy endowed with such cunning and magnificence, the kind that as I write this chapter has already a contingency of one or more of its agents within your own body in the form of micro plastics, or plastic production derived toxins, mercury and more. We really do not know what they are doing at present but they are already there and in most of the animal food we eat.

The declaration of war against CEGE is not just inevitable but unavoidable in the age of life. The auspicious recognition of a Compounded Environmental Global Effect or CEGE, radically changes the picture of the partitioned and further fragmented environmental front, its measures, targets and concerns, but above all, CEGE identifies an enemy of life on Earth at a scale, reach and vitality that only a concerted effort like war and all of its dedicated forces, can aspire to deliver life on earth to safer grounds.

Who else but the world's armies are fit, disciplined, organized, loyal to a chain of command, housed, fed and funded to begin to respond and to do what they have done for millennia, namely to reinvent themselves and develop the right weapons for the right targets, to deploy and to carry missions attacking at the discretion of well advised leaders and their commanding officers.

You will also notice that the institution of war and its entire armature is not only conserved but also greatly expanded, the only difference is the kind of enemy they will engage. That is all; we no longer have to send our children to kill or be killed by the children of other parents. This is where a culture of world peace operating under these circumstances will have its greatest impact as humanity rallies behind its troops with all of our children fighting on the same mission, fighting for the right of life on Earth, to remain on course in the age of life.

Conventional war as we know it was a Holocene phenomenon that has no place in the age of life even if violence will be a remnant impulse for a long time, that is if we decide to move away from the path to extinction. Of course if we do not and stay on the current course, the inevitable fall of the super powers and the fierce fight for the last pockets of energy and other resources will unleash a chain of events harboring a rein of horrific carnage leading to the time when CEGE finally claims the rest of the Earth's biosphere.

In the age of life however, war can still be war and the institutional imperative that designs and controls war will have no trouble evolving to suit conditions so long as there is a war to be fought and revenues to be made from it, after all that is what war has always been about, besides, the war against CEGE will likely last for centuries and so would its revenues. Happily the war against CEGE is a winnable war because we know the enemy, we created it and we can destroy it.

The campaign against CEGE is a war where we can pour the intellectual capital of humanity, as never before and for the first time in history, do so for life, on behalf of all humanity and the world.

One can only imagine the concerted effort carried out by the sciences to devise strategies and for the design of noble systems and applications for the new armed forces of the world with their distinct missions and strategy against CEGE.

All of this activity is played out, under basically the same patronage structure, with better funding with public support and without the need to invoke inhumanity to own kind in the design criteria. This time around, intelligence will refer to the human capacity to rationalize problems and on that, science would have a lot to do in the identification of targets and the tactical detail required to disarm them.

In this war the culture of war will team up with the culture of world peace to invest their individual resources in the combined effort, to forge a new reality for humanity in the age of life.

Could that talk be just delusional or just the stuff of another empty dream?

Neither, in fact the only way that the war machine will get to keep its stipends will be largely because an active culture of world peace grows parallel to the war initiative. Further, as the culture of peace own economic base grows, the culture of peace should be able to invest and sponsor the focus and stability of a collective society to the mission.

Mean while, a multitude of new economic opportunities and jobs that never existed before will surface; their appearance will in terms, help to prop up the social wants and deficits that currently perpetuate violence in its many forms around the world.

One has to consider the sheer power of the motivation behind the "age of life" banner and how it can be embraced by a civilization that has really not much left to believe in and nothing really new to dream about.

History shows time and time again, that if you give people a reason that they can believe in, the difficult tasks are readily accomplished and the impossible ones take just a little longer but they get done. We conquered the world didn't we!

You may perhaps be concerned, with the thought about how are we going to be persuaded to turn our attention away from the current conflicts between nations, between religious beliefs, between political persuasions and their special interest between corporate concerns of consumption and conservation and between the self-interest of the ruling class and the needs of the people.

Moreover, the innumerable conflicts between the divided and subdivided masses who's programed anguish prevents them from rising to the surface of reality to see the transparency of the innocent, but cruel agenda of control over their cognitive map and what they think, kept away from what they should be thinking by the necessity of an institutional imperative that cannot work any other way.

These are all very real tensions indeed, their combined energy, led our cultural Holocene advance toward the gradual deterioration of civilization, of humanity and of the world's environment, but those are tensions that are eased by the reality of the Anthropocene landscape and the narrow path left by the prospects of extinction to the continuation of more of the same.

The truth is that all of those concerns really mean nothing in the face of a general collapse of the entire system where the death of the elite or of the lowest class would not be noticed because there would not be anyone left to do so.

Conversely, the addition of the real need and want for life that no one seems to object, a fact that is demonstrated by the almost fanatic reach for youth and vitality by our current society, which seems to indicate, that the addition of the concerns about life itself, to the operative equation of all of civilization, would in the short-term, begin to ameliorate the severity of the issues mentioned and their capacity to sustain legitimate reasons for their continuation.

Furthermore, the focus on life and the support to the war against CEGE would help to replace shallow short terms ambitions, for long-term objectives that bear greater rewards whilst pointing to life as the asset with the greater value.

It follows, that with the advent of a culture of world peace in the Anthropocene, a peculiar observation has surfaced and that is that war is linked to death and peace is linked to life but while they are opposite polarities, it is their simultaneous and combined energy, which creates the effect of balance and stability that can run the cultural engine of civilization better for all parties involved.

That peculiar observation has never really been made because on close inspection, humanity never really included life itself as a critical factor in any of its mayor ideas. Had we done so, violence would have never become the leading indicator of civilization and the demise of the global biosphere would not be the barometer measuring the deficit caused by the absence of life itself as a priority; but it is.

Data-A aesthetics has dramatically demonstrated that point by extending art into life and unifying their energies to stabilize meaning in terms of life itself.

It follows that, as we take this narrative back to the war in the age of life, we can begin to see a fresh vitality rising where all we could see before where the prospects of doom behind the hopelessness of more of the same.

In the war against CEGE the extension of war into peace for the unification of their energies would effectively create a kind of Life-Power-Cell of such magnificence so as to power humanity to fight the war of wars, in the age of life.

Well, let's take a look at a sampler of the battles that our new Life-Power-Cell can energize.

As the culture of world peace expands around the world, so does the message about the nature, the need and the mutual benefits that human collectivity around the world can bestow on behalf of the war initiative against CEGE. Likewise, so can at the same time the military forces of the world begin to examine the collective value of a global concentration of power that may be sufficient to as they say, take down CEGE.

Please keep steadily in mind, that this is quite a real scenario that is a part of our conscious migration, which is also tempered by the new reality as it develops in the Anthropocene epoch and into the age of life. I grant you that these matters are more complicated than that but fundamentally, that is about what it would take to do it.

What that means is that the culture of world peace moves forward to demonstrate the validity of global collectivity in the building of the spirit behind humanity's support for the war in the age of life and how such support clears the way for the offensive against CEGE to become a realistic idea.

Under the global banner of "the age of life," the might of a collective global military force may begin to be assembled and the offensive against CEGE can begin.

Just imagine all of the naval forces of the world given the charge of clean up and restoration of the world's Oceans, the mobilization of millions of civilians of every level of specialization to new jobs in retrofitting war vessels and building the new environmental weaponry to enable millions of newly retrained enlisted personnel to carry-out the task and the millions of people on land busy in new jobs processing, disarming and redirecting the toxic captured materials to be made by millions more into new products for new uses that will secure their imprisonment.

Imagine the air forces running support and coordination to support the naval efforts and more importantly, their part in the mission to rid the earth of human induced radioactive materials, for which the air forces and the space agencies would need to plan, design, build and deploy spacecraft and orbital facilities capable of assembling train-like aggregations of containers with radioactive materials to be sent to the sun for final disposal.

Curiously the development of the system and facilities to do that will find its training grounds in the clean up of space debris, its capture, processing and deployment to the sun. Another mission with millions of new jobs and new technological advances attached to it.

Add on to that the ground forces of the world's armies, and you have the clean up and restoration of the land, the rivers, water, conservation and the ecosystems of the world.

I'm sure you got the big picture by now and can imagine how all of this plays down from the highest offices to the lowest post of civilization and from the largest creature to the smallest. Therefore I will stop here because it gets better the deeper one peruses into the transformation of one of the oldest human institutions, to the fulfillment of the original purpose for which it was created in the first place before greed and the thirst for power took it over, to safeguard and protect the city (civilization) from the attack of invading enemy forces and the restoration of a world that has done nothing but be giving to our wants and tolerant to our innocence.

War in the age of life is more than a beautiful metaphor that gives meaning to the banner for the age of life, it is a real choice that lays at our front door, it is the gift that the culture of world peace bequeaths civilization trough the new reality so that our migrating journey in this new world as hard as it will be at first can have the incentive of a real goal ahead and a real outcome that can be a measure of the power of the human mind to embrace life itself as its greatest asset.

"A War for Life"

Chapter XIV
Leading the war

The culture of war is the most widely documented history of humanity in fact it is basically the entire history of civilization. It is a phenomenal tale of wholesale violence for wholesale greed in an ambitious effort to dominate the world and everything in it; however big the world was at the time that some king or someone felt the need to have it all, under his rule.

Curiously, history also shows that while there have been many empires; the greedy impulse that built them is unfortunately the same impulse that brought them down.

I mention that arguable fact merely to point out at the procession of people in power over the millennia, that led their people to war, did so, under the auspice of a developing culture of war, which had instituted "violence" within civilization, as the exclusive means of control and expansion of their domains.

It must be noticed that when the only choice is violence, all of the culture in a civilized society would have the tendency to revolve around violence as it still does at present time. That is in a nutshell human civilization during the Holocene epoch.

The Anthropocene epoch, or better yet, the age of life, begins with a heavy load of cultural trauma that accumulated over thousands of years, which coupled with newly inflicted injuries constitute the narrative of the thousands of grievances that plague human relations and that are the source of so much pain and suffering around the world. They are recurring grievances that are refreshed with new incidents to create the experiences that preserve their emotional content to be transferred to the next generation.

However, the presence of a culture of peace, goes a long way to mitigate these long standing grievances in the Anthropocene, beginning with the reality that violence is no longer the only choice because violence is now clearly half of the equation with peace being the other half. Moreover the war/peace equation now has "life" as a common denominator and the survival of the species as its ultimate goal.

CEGE is not after fame and glory, is not after conquest or power, is not after anyone's money, status, property, social standing or believes; CEGE is after life itself, yours, whomever you are and includes all other plants, animals in the world. As I said before; CEGE is the human-made-spirit of the 6th mass extinction event on Earth.

I have always admired the dissidents, the activists and the intellectuals throughout history because they always held up a mirror, upon which, the extent of our human incompleteness as beings was revealed, particularly to the horror of the people whom the culture itself, had burdened with the directives to do wrong.

Happily in the age of life, dissidents, activists and intellectuals will finally take their place within the human collective, their vision and wisdom becoming a critical part of the solution and dissidence will take on a new meaning.

Human dissidents in the age of life would have to favor CEGE's values and objectives against all life, their own included and that is insanity, as life itself has no living dissidents and therefore dissidence is not a tool in the Anthropocene.

I have been trying to establish a scenario where our collective focus on life itself as seen from a position in which we humanity, can accept the fact that the way forward is dramatically influenced by our embrace of all life and its conservation, as the central aim and motivation behind the war initiative against CEGE and life as the guiding objective leading the war.

The title for this chapter came up inspired by the emotional and cultural impact that a slogan like the "age of life" could have, in inspiring an entire species with so much to loose and so much more to gain to allow the very thing that is slipping away, namely life, to be the highest office leading the war.

To my mind, other than CEGE, there is no power on earth that is at odds with life itself, nor is there a human institution or human being that is independent of life and there is not a shred of evidence anywhere on this earth, which shows that life is not the main concern of all of the creatures in the world.

So when I suggest that regardless of all of the grievances and differences, in spite of our errors and blunders, that withstanding the horrors of our inhumanity to our own kind, gathering under the banner of the age of life in this new world, places humanity at the start of a new vision for our species and at the door of an understanding, that the reasons we held against each other in the past, somehow already fulfilled their promise and because their fulfillment has only brought pain, destruction, horror and despair, there is no reason to continue to insist that some how they will service a need that no longer exists.

In the confluence of all human history into the state and status of a single species whose best chance for survival lies in collectivity, no one needs to be overthrown no one group needs to be eliminated, no institution destroyed and no one needs dramatic chance; all however will need to evolve and carry their best ideas to the inclusion of life itself as the trusted source of meaning and guidance.

In the Holocene epoch, we borrowed from each other to create the cultural context that however incomplete is all we have moving forward, this time we will have Nature to advise us and life leading the war.

Nice words but how are we actually going to get together to do this?

Well, the question answers itself, as the reality is that we are already together, we may not be unified as a species but that is only a choice and for the most part choices are made in a matter of minutes when situations demand that a choice be made.
Furthermore there may be 10 million other species numbering in the trillions of beings that are already unified in the ranks of life already standing by, there is a natural global process ready for reassignment to service in the campaign against CEGE.

We are however, already wired together by the Internet and information, the right information can be in front of the eyes and ears of billions of people within minutes when we want that to happen.

Now, as the ruling class of humanity is advised that their place is secure because this battle is not against them, but against a common enemy and that as their understanding on the matter deepens, their critical role spelled out, their rule would be seen as indispensible by all, within the new reality. After all, they know how to rule, they just never ruled with life in their sights, nor did they ever, had the admiration of the world for their rule, as they become the true patrons of the war initiative against CEGE and take their place at the pinnacle of the culture of world peace.

There has never been anything wrong with class differences, so long as all of them have life itself as their mutual common denominator and the respect as members of the same species, so long as all share with dignity their right to be alive, to have sufficient food, shelter, and a livelihood with a measure of happiness and pride in what they do to contribute to the whole. Nature is the master teacher for class studies.

Remember that the shoemaker that makes the soldier's boots is the soldier's hero in the battlefield for the comfort they provide in each and every step. A bit corny but hope you get the point.

However, in the Anthropocene, class is what it was supposed to be all along, meaning, an attribute of distinction between the various skills and functions of the citizenry, all of which contribute to the fulfillment of the operation and well-being of the human society.

Moving on, with the ruling class on board, Government is also advised that no overthrow, revolution or radical changes need to be a concern, because in the age of life, reason is reinforced by a new reality and that reality would consider Holocene notions of overthrow and so on, as well intended repetitions of a technique that has never worked on the long run. It is like the removal of a deficient but working vital organ like a kidney, replaced by another, which we think may work better while tearing the rest of the body apart in the course of the operation. Does that ring a historical bell for you?

Government will see the wisdom of the new reality an follow the example of the ruling class to the real advantages that come with a plan, a doable solution scenario that they did not have to come up with, but that they can easily adopt because the cultural instruments that drive the campaign revitalizes their original role in society. Meanwhile the growing culture of peace gradually helps to remove, the heavy burdens of control through violence and misinformation while opening the door for a renewed public trust in government as the steward of life in the city, state or nation.

The big Industry and the special interest crowd will also follow closely as there is no reason to weaken the very entity that will lead the way to the manufacture and production of the environmental weapons for the war against CEGE and capitalize on the technological renaissance of repurposing the disarmed CEGE troops.

On the contrary, big industry would be able to go public and announce honestly that their special interest can include the interest of life in their bottom line and that their corporations and conglomerates will also benefit greatly from not only the campaign against CEGE but from the growing culture of world peace and the millions of people whose labor and enthusiasm to the task, enjoys their respect and sufficient remuneration. Big industry will discover Sustainable Continuity and see the wisdom of long-term stability in the age of life.

Similarly, the religions of the world would not be able to avoid the contemplation of what is by human standards in any age, a miracle in the making, humanity is in an exodus from an age of war, intolerance, hate, and wanton destruction of a benign and wonderful world, towards a new conscious level of their humanity as the species embrace its adulthood and begins its new great migration in the age of life.

The impulse of religion has not been understood
any better than science has understood life, those
youthful squabbles between religious devotees
and atheists would be better advised to consider
that those rather unproductive encounters are
Holocene preoccupations weighed with a lot of
innocence on both sides, as neither argument has
had a proof and what is most likely to happen, is
that the proof will tend to validate both
arguments in the new reality.

Still, so long as there are more than five billion
people responding to the impulse of religion or
mysticism and while the appointed keepers of the
impulse continue to respond to their presence in
the sacred places, the presence of a culture of
world peace in their lives will be read as a sign
that religion too must also be a part of the
migration initiative and that their vision too will
be tempered by the new reality in the age of life.

Science has always played a vital an important
role in decoding nature and adapting the natural
discourse to our own purpose and design in a
systematic way, to construct the body of facts and
truths that constitute human nature, with nature
seen as no more than a commodity whose laws of
operation play conveniently well in the advance
of our quest to conquer everything.

That is perhaps a flippant but fair overview of
science in the Holocene, a field zealous of

honesty, inflexible about hypothesis and proof and heavily guarded against hear say, but, life itself, never quite entered even its popular definition nor was Nature commonly acknowledged as the master template from which our best approximations came from.

In the war against CEGE however, Science will have to evolve to embrace Nature not merely as its subject matter, but as the wiser teacher and life itself as the faculty provost. Science has a lot to undo to disarm CEGE and an awful lot to create to arm humanity against it in the age of life.

The media would have one of the most critical roles to play in the entire campaign, once the coast is cleared for them to return to being the voice of the people and no longer the mouthpiece of a kind of institutional imperative that is dismissive of the truth and cherry-picks the facts for convenience. Harsh as it sounds, that too, was a Holocene imposition by the culture, a heavy burden on countless able people and a disgrace to the ideals of freedom of expression.

The arts are being mentioned here last, not because they are less important in this context but because as an artist I chose to defer to the other institutions as a gesture of respect even though in the social totem pole there is a tendency for the arts to be last, particularly in education, as free thinking and creativity of thought and people with fresh ideas of their own, have been for obvious reasons, considered to be a greatly undesirable inconvenience in the Holocene epoch.

As for the arts themselves, they also befell the burden of the culture and perhaps if not more so than the other institutions, its visibility in the world made it the more conspicuous as the late great art critic Robert Hughes describes it:

"One could say that the arts somehow mirrors the decadence of the world – nonsense – it is decadent itself, it has no critical function; it is part of the problem. The art world usually copies the money driven celebrity obsessed entertainment culture, falling for the same fixation on fame, same obedience to mass media who jostles for our attention with its wows of flash and flutter."

In the age of life, art will have to do much better and happily it is, this is a work of art and I'm not alone on the production of the first examples of Anthropocene art, all of which will certainly contribute to convey the message of the age to all of humanity as we have seen. The contrast between Data-A art and the art of the Holocene is unmistakable.

By way of example let me share a thought from one of the newest stars in the art firmament that goes by the name of "Banksy" from the book by the same name and expressing the fervor of street art; he says. "The system is corrupt and therefore anyway we can attack it is legitimate." Conversely, the Data-A appraisal of the system within the new reality would be; "The system may be corrupt, however, the legitimate thing to do is to help to improve it anyway we can."

I personally admire Banksy's work, but I cannot admire the irreverence of a tactic that becomes a part of the problem when it should not be.

Fortunately that too may change soon and I hope it does, because public street art is much more than that as I demonstrated that point with "Diffusion Billboard Opus 1982," where the system was moved to create the art in public places ordinance and where even the police came to the site to offer protection and even food, as I worked day and night in the open street, surrounding with street art what is now the justice center in Fort Myers Florida.

More dramatically perhaps is the case of the Chinese dissident Ai Waiwai whom I greatly admire and fully respect his work, but again Data-A prescribes that instead of flat out protest and the consequences that go with it, art can now create models of solutions and improvements on behalf of the system one wishes to improve and whose performance may actually generate the changes as even the most irascible way of governance will go with the one idea that gives it the most convenience and performance. After all, the truth about humanity is that we did not know what else to do, but we do now.

I have up to this moment in this chapter, mentioned a number of key institutions of civilization and their direct relevance to the war initiative against CEGE, but I do not have to remind you, that at the chore of all of them are people and at the foundation of civilization itself are people. It is people from all walks of life who make the whole idea of humanity work and unfortunately it is also people who lost their connection to this basic fact, who have made life so difficult for everyone and have placed all of life in jeopardy.

Still, it is people who no matter how divided and marginalized by class, by race, by color, by culture and all of the rest, we all get up each day to respond to our calling as best we can, regardless of how informed or misinformed we are regarding the state of the world.

Nevertheless, we may all of us, be castaways of the Holocene epoch, but we are not stranded in this new world, here in this Anthropocene epoch we are all just people again and a great many of us already know, that whatever plans you have for the future, they are not going to happen without water, air and edible food.

Once again and this time knowingly, we are a single species again and as such we stand to win.

So who is leading the war?

We are, all of us, the human species where everyone is people and in this battle there should not be an idle hand or a missing talent or a bit of culture that is not a part of this effort, as the old Chinese saying goes; "a grain of rice can tip the scales" and as I have said repeatedly we have Nature on our side and the best motivation that a species can have at the start of a long campaign is; Life itself.

"Cultural Evolution"

Chapter XV
Leading the cultural evolution – recovery

In this chapter, we will have to recall at least
minimally the extent of the real general crisis
attending our prospects for survival as discussed
earlier in previous chapters, which as cursory as
the examination was, nonetheless left us with no
doubt that we are not only in real trouble but in a
new world altogether indeed.

Further, as the idea of recovery is invoked, the
global landscape of what is to be recovered
comes into view and the enormity of the recovery
effort itself, present us with a picture of
something so dramatic, that the scene is more
akin to the aftermath of a war by our species
against the planet itself.

Add to that, a history that is also peppered by
wars against our own kind around the world from
which the destruction of cities and ways of life
are not only visible but where the smoke is still
rising.

If that wasn't enough, our species has been
plagued with what seems to be a perpetual feud
against ourselves, within the borders of our own
families, our own neighborhoods, our work place,
our government, our own diversity of ideas and
expression, our laws and so on down an
interminable list that has made us all strangers in

our own land, strangers to humanity, strangers to Nature and to all other life; no wonder every other creature runs away from us on sight.

It follows that as history shows, that kind of feud or hostility and war has been going on for thousands of years to where the word "recovery" may not the best choice in our case because clearly there is not a previous state or ideal model of coexistence to be regained or reestablish, as the meaning of the word recovery implies, at least within the span of our human experience with civilization.

Therefore, the reason I named the chapter; "Leading the cultural evolution – recovery," is because the concept of recovery does suit the natural component of the environmental problem, which has indeed a prior state of sufficiency to recover or regain and cultural evolution is perfectly suitable for the human component of the problem which as we have seen, has no serviceable prior in sight.

Now, as our main concern with both components mentioned, is their combined and mutual survival in sustainable continuity on planet Earth, then we can conclude that human cultural evolution is the best alternative to more of the same, which is something no one can possibly desire now that the cultural instruments to do so are already here.

I will argue that a journalist would be hard pressed to get from an interview with someone from the ruling elite, from a sitting president, from a religious leader, from an industrialist or a serious intellectual, a statement that reads something like…

"Taking in consideration the fact that there is a better way forward for humanity and realizing that the only real thing that we stand to lose is our ignorance about life and its new possibilities; I really think that staying on the course to collapse and the end of all that we have worked for and the possible extinction of all life on earth, is the best thing to do regardless of the opportunity to evolve culturally and survive."

No one is going to be up for collective suicide in the face of a real way out, as what is being suggested here, is the result of a lifetime of studying the problem and the path that the work opens is nature tested, the ideas may look humble in their human infancy but they are as old as time and as old as life on earth.

Besides it is not I who would lead the human cultural evolution and the recovery of our natural world, but culture itself aided by the cultural tools that reinforce humanity's general cultural context.

Of course it is a fact, that human culture resides in its people and therefore the cultural evolutionary front is people from all walks of life and from every level of society, who are learning to incorporate life itself in the criteria of their own specialty while adapting their specialty to the recovery of nature in our world.

Human cultural evolution does not require any kind of revolution or the mandate of force driven laws or any other Holocene measures that where implemented in the absence of cultural instruments capable of addressing the questions of what to do and how to do it.

For human cultural evolution to begin, we need only to take a good look at what we have become as humans, at what we have done to the world and at our prospects for survival on the current course.

We have kept each other at a distance long enough, but no more, the old reasons for our differences are no longer reasons in the eyes of the new reality and the new reality is here to see us come together for an unavoidable good reason, our world is collapsing like a house of cards and life is coming down with it.

But, how are we going to get everybody to even think about cultural evolution when the whole of society is so fractured and at odds with each other?

There is but one simple answer to that, we do it the same way we did it at the beginning of civilization, because as sophisticated as we may think we are, we are still operating by the same basic principles and we are still organized largely the same way.

Therefore, allow me to suggest that the leadership of the cultural evolution, is the concerted effort that is to be orchestrated by the command of the ruling elite and their appointment of the five organizing agencies of human civilization, namely, Government, the Sciences, industry, religion, and media to the task of cultural evolution; with the addition of Nature as the fiduciary for all life within the earth's biosphere and with the patronage of all of the people in the world participating as a single species, in relative peace with each other and the world but at war against the known enemy of life occurring in the form of CEGE.

Admittedly, the wording may look kind of funny but I believe, that this is the first time that paragraph has ever been written, however, if you take a close look at it through the lens of history, you will notice the striking similarity in principle, with the leadership that set us off, in the conquest of the world and for the development of the culture that made it happen and that brought us to this new world.

 We do not have to fight to convince anybody to get this done, it may not begin immediately but we know that the higher you go on the social scale the more informed everyone is and because the facts are inescapable, everyone knows what is going on, all of the misinformation, sidestepping and denial of the facts as reprehensible as they are, to my mind they are not the result of ignorance of the facts, or of deliberate mal intention, they are like anything else human in the Holocene epoch, the direct product and effect of a culture at the boundary of its capacity to resolve a problem that no one expected, because the culture could not have foreseen something that did not exist.

But now the problem and all of its attributes do exist and the culture has to rise to its challenges and that is why I'm optimistic that the leadership that I invoked above will step forward to save the day by doing what we have always done albeit a little different in application but largely the same in principle.

As I said many times before Humanity does not really have to change, it only needs to evolve, as the combination of Anthropocene pressures mount, the emergence of a culture of world peace, the discovery of new organizational natural first principles, the addition of two unifying perspectives and their adaptation as cultural instruments, constitute a cultural evolutionary trigger that effectively updates the human cultural context in line with the demands of the new Anthropocene world.

And just in case that you may be thinking that I have forgotten about the thousands of organizations devoted to bring change to thousands of critical human and environmental issues, you would be mistaken, as no single entity has the breath or the investigative scope of some of these organizations in their specific area of interest. Their individual and collective import to the cultural evolution is vital and their motivation on their membership base, a crucial via for diffusion of the pertinent information.

If you had a feeling that the labors of millions of activists throughout history and the many contemporary voices of intellectuals who at great pains an personal risk have diligently become veritable human encyclopedic libraries of facts in their proper historical place and whose knowledge may no longer be marginalized but rather enlisted as vital unbiased critical reference, that will inform the leadership of cultural evolution, where the Holocene cultural land mines are and perhaps even how to disarm them.

I saved my comments on the activism of various people and groups for last in this chapter about the leadership of human cultural evolution, because it must be made as clear as possible that, while it is an undeniable fact that throughout the entire history of civilization or even of humanity itself, there have always been people whose intelligence and keen focus on the affairs of humanity, made them into observers of the reality of life in their midst.

They where and still are, people who have made a concerted effort to understand the effects of human culture on society and the peculiar contrasts between classes and how their differences, constituted a society divided by degrees of power and subject to the rigors of cultural prescriptions where an ever widening gap of inequality lessens the relationship between people as people.

That unfortunate isthmus is a Holocene cultural deficiency, that has been a source of not only the bulk of human unhappiness but the main source of all of the grievances that plague civilization and that have polarized humanity into the us and them setting off the perpetual riff that activists and intellectuals have addressed for thousands of years.

In the Anthropocene world humanity reaches adulthood and the adult humanity has no time for the us-versus-them as CEGE would claim both with no knowledge or concern for their pretend differences.

The adult humanity is therefore obliged to equality with distinction for individual and collective qualifications, to the roles, which need to be played to sustain the human project alive, with sufficiency in the allocation of resources that sustain the livelihood of all living things, with the dignity that embraces their contribution to the whole; as key to the collective reality of the adult humanity.

The primitive impulse of power as amplified by the human species never really had a chance to learn about power from Nature, but now it has a chance. By way of illustration, as you know, our sun is the most powerful agent in his solar system and yet the sun uses its power to power life, here on earth, the smallest creatures like the single celled protozoan Euglena, lowly in the web of life, but able to see the sun, draws all of the sunlight it needs while the largest creatures do the same; all of life is reverent to the sun and yet the sun is just content to power life. That is absolute power!

Power in the Anthropocene will be renewed to a higher state by the influence of the new reality and the cultural evolution it engenders. It is to that power, that the voices and the wisdom of the activist and the intellectuals will be a most welcome counsel, this is true, because the campaign to keep life on earth cannot do without those who track life and know the places where only power can foster life and well-being with a measure of happiness.

I have been frequently challenged by close observers who note that humanity is much to fragmented, polarized and at odds with itself to ever take a minute to consider, little less act, on this kind of lofty designs of unity an cultural evolution.

My response has always been, well, while that may be true and the actual conditions may be even worse than we have imagined, which I think they are, there is a point where denial and stubbornness break down and where in the same quiet places that decisions are made to stay the course and get the world for all that is worth, life also titters there and while there may be banks too big to fail, there is no such a thing as a man too rich to die.

And if by chance greed is so inclined to try to take it all, then we are in good shape because the best part of the human project lies in the Anthropocene where the decision to embrace the age of life would bring a kind of wealth that has never even been imagined by human minds.

Evolve and conquer!

"The Vision"

Chapter XVI
A vision of the new humanity

Looking into the future is a very tricky affair, but not if you have data, pertinent data from reliable sources, Nature and life being my favorite sources, with human sciences and general human history bringing the comparative analog as human nature.

This book, is for us the human kind of course and wanting to see into the future has been a preoccupation for as long as the concept of future creped into our menu of ideas with interesting and mysterious things to be said. So thinking about the future, is nothing new, however thinking about a new humanity would at first glance, be considered more science fiction than actually peeking into the future, that is, as far as the future can be seen.

In this chapter, A vision of the new humanity, however, is more of an appraisal of possibilities that depend greatly on how soon and how successful we are in beginning our conscious and cultural migration towards a tomorrow of our own making in partnership with nature and at peace with the world.

The green path, which I referenced before as a perspective, is a field that has a lot more to offer than meets the eye, it will require a separate book to just open the dialog of what is really a marvelous story about life on Earth, from which I have to take a snippet to make a point for this chapter.

The green path, in a nutshell, is the story of life on earth as best as we know it including an episode where at a point six million years ago, one of its creatures "homo" departs from Nature to create a nature of its own and after a short period, geologically speaking, the budding nature that one of its descendants; Homo sapiens, inherits from its antecedents is pushed forward to become Homo sapiens sapiens or the independent force of nature that is us "wise wise human;" so to speak.

With remarkable wit and technology the human creature conquers the world, but the reign is short lived and by the beginning of the 21st century, in its own calendar, the wise human being begins to understand that being wise is not the same as having wisdom. That fact is realized by our species, at the prospects of a collapsed world environment by our own hand and at the horror of the realization that on our present course, we are soon to be another evolutionary dead end.

It follows, that the green path allows for an independent view by Nature itself, of our beginning where our departure from the natural path to our present position, can be tracked, whilst Nature and the rest of life stayed on the natural course. Think about that for a moment...

What was one path for billions of years became bifurcated or forked into two paths, one, the robust and diversified path of millions of separate species walking through time on the same path, unified with their Nature, the other, a tiny path barely visible on the time scale of life on Earth, walked by the bipedal creature that became us, isolated from the world and wise enough to destroy Nature and its own kind in the relative innocence of its adolescence as a species.

It is at this point where, what I mean by a vision of the new humanity can or should begin to make sense, because we are at a junction in the history of Earth where two geological epochs meet and where one of them will determine the future of life on earth.

We have to keep in mind that Nature will go on with or without us and that planet Earth has something that we do not have and that is lots of time. Nature on earth has seen five mass extinctions events so that the one we are on is not news to Nature, we may have irreparably damaged the original recipe of life here, but nature is all about recipes and something else will come up, but not with us included there.

For a vision of the new humanity, the Anthropocene is the place where we begin to walk toward Nature with the idea of rejoining the common path of life; what I call the Green Path. When I say we, however, I mean all of us with all of our history, our ideas, our Gods our diversity our triumphs, our blunders, our rich, our poor and so on...

All of that is the human species and at the beginning of our return to nature, which is why, this book is called "The Next Great Migration" no one I can think of, is so wise as to ascertain just what to take or leave behind, so the best thing is to bring all our history.

A number of years ago, I was amazed to read in the scientific literature about what the geneticists of the day called "junk DNA" and what the new generation of geneticists marvel in the DNA, as the most comprehensive data conservation system ever found with the entire history of life on Earth to be found in just four letters.

We created a human nature of our own and that nature has to go with us towards the reunion with Nature, especially now that we are the only ones who can undo some of our worst concoctions we created and who have the ability to do things that life cannot do in unnatural time scales.

The cultural evolutionary path that our new cultural instruments sponsor will help us to select and adapt our present cultural context to the needs and exigencies of life as we move forward. The early part of the migration will be the hardest as we are late in declaring war against CEGE and equally tardy in establishing a culture of world peace, which is the only resistance we have against CEGE as we know that only a collective effort by all of humanity will do the trick.

A vision of a new humanity at least one with substance, know-how, direction, goals and the incentive that life, fuller than we ever imagined is already there, in fact it is here now but we have not yet learned to see it.

A vision like that is, I hope for the sake of life, a most enticing alternative to what we have at present and the prospects that attend it, a new vision for ourselves and the world is perhaps the closest we, as a species, will ever come to see a way to realize the ancient impulse to migrate towards a promised land of our and Nature collective making.

Cultural evolution as suggested here is migration of a sort and I dare say, that it should be considered also as a trigger for human biological evolution, as a change in the cognitive capacity of a species has got to, on the long run sponsor biological changes in the brain and on the process synthesis of the human biology.

I mention evolution only because it must be pointed out to all of those people who favor revolution and the overthrow of existing structures of power, that revolution does not and never has improved the cognitive capacity of the people who replace the ousted structures of power, they merely assume a role, which as history shows, not only perpetuates violence and hatred but culturally dooms the new order to do the same even though by different means.

Therefore, the key is culture and a cultural shift with life itself as its primary focus, as seen from the vantage point of humanity at present, demands cultural evolution and furthermore, cultural evolution cannot happen without a fresh vision of humanity and the possible means to achieve it.

So we come to the point, where the only peek into the future to be had from here at the Holocene Anthropocene junction is, that our cultural evolution during our passage through the Anthropocene towards our reunion with Nature and the world, will turn our species, into the real custodians of all life on earth. Chances are that when that happens, which I hope it does, the human that will enter the reunion would not be us, it will be a human evolved from us, but it will be a different human who will establish; a new humanity in the recovered landscape of the new world.

I have perhaps presumptuously named this new human "Homo sapiens integralis" only because what else would you call a human that after a six million year absence from the green path, rejoins it as a co-creator of the ensuing direction of life in the planet; in unison with nature.

An "integral human" which is what the name means, is therefore a possibility and only because it is part of a vision that is for all practical purposes probable, now, what makes it probable is not what is being offered here alone, but because the vision falls within a body of data, or information in human hands, that already peeked into the private sanctum of life.

That data, is a survey, which not really knowing, prepared the species to embrace life itself, beyond the reaches of a Holocene cultural context, albeit not beyond a landscape of reality of such magnificence, which hopefully will compel those possessing the data, not to turn their back on the very Nature that so obligingly bestowed the data on humanity to begin with.

A vision for a new humanity is therefore a transport vehicle for a species that has to evolve or perish, a vision for a humanity who has paved the way here, with the blood of their own kind, all in exchange for a paper kingdom that now clamors for all life as it crumbles down.

Of course is just a vision take it or leave it, the thing is, that not considering its breath and possibility would make it very difficult indeed for any rational being to profess love to their children or to prefer to crawl into a familiar bubble and pretend the vision is not there, not now that we are so close to the beginning of a meaningful migration or to the end of another story in the history of life.

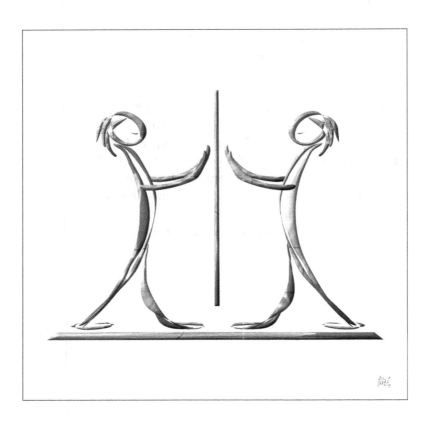

"First Law of Law"

Chapter XVII
The principles of tomorrow

It is funny that we come to the last chapter, only to find, that the chapter is all about beginning, which is essentially what the word "principle" means and goes on from there to gather additional significance in relation to truth, law in the human context or to natural law as in the elemental aspects of how the universe works.

The migration initiative that I have endeavor to outline here in this book is a beginning of many beginnings, it is a beginning of our adulthood as a species, it is the beginning of our identity as a single species, it is the beginning of our reunion with Nature and the world, it is the beginning of our mission as custodians of life on Earth, it is also the beginning of our culture of world peace and the beginning of the first war where our weapons are not pointed to another human being.

Each of those beginnings entails a certain amount of effort and perseverance, but they need only to be embraced by our individual and collective conscious to begin and to gain a foothold in the real world, with real consequences to our lives.

Likewise each one of those beginnings bequeaths great dividends, prominent amongst is the arrest and stabilization of the mass extinction event that is in progress, which brings me to the most critical and the most sanguine of our beginnings, namely, the beginning of our individual and collective love affair with life itself.

There we have in life itself a first principle that cannot be denied by anything or anyone living, as life is the beginning of all beginnings upon which, each living thing is a continuation of a kind of flow-force that lends its energy, to the construction of marvelous living tapestries like the one on Earth, living tapestries which are richly embroidered with a diversity of creatures made from a single thread, who survive under the sun over the surface of a living planet like ours.

So, there we have a principle that suggests that life in this universe is the peculiar continuation of a beginning that is dramatized by a series of subsequent beginnings, whose duration is the experience of being alive, an experience which is passed on in continuity for the duration of the universe.

In other words, we could think of life (organic and elemental) as a continuous process of exchange of the original (beginning) energy in a given universe.

Anyway, I made mention of life like that, so as to suggest that there is a lot more to life than meets the eyes at present and that before we turn our attention and focus to life itself, it is wise to acknowledge that larger truth, as we enter the new world with all of its demands knowing that life is the key if we are going to survive.

Of course I had to save for last, the most obvious of the new beginnings, but also the one beginning with the most critical challenges coming from many sources and affecting many different areas of civilization including the world's environment.

I'm talking about the beginning of our experience with life in the Anthropocene epoch.

By way of illustration, allow me to relate to that beginning with the story of a few people who decide to restore life on an empty lot in the middle of a big city, which had become a dumping ground for all sorts of garbage, big, unwieldy, toxic, dangerous to remove, rat infested and so on, add on to that difficulty the fact that the actual owners of the lot do not want the lot restored claiming future plans for it, before long the people appealed to the city on health and safety reasons that the lot be cleaned up and turned into at least a temporary community garden where the children can see life grow and so on. You notice that nothing has been done on the lot and already there are lots of problems to solve, when the actual clean up begins all kinds of new problems pop up, how to remove and dispose of the garbage, followed by the refurbishing of the soil to make it suitable for planting, followed by the actual planting and upkeep of the garden and so on...

That is what we have to do with the whole planet but with a lot more problems than landlord, city laws and labor, we have big problems because we changed the world so much. It is a beginning but it will be a beginning whose hardships can be alleviated by the gifts of all of the other beginnings I have mentioned in the age of life.

There is however a principle that is quite common in Nature and widely used by life on earth which when translated for use by human culture, may offer an interesting and welcome dividend in matters where only abstract notions have prevailed until now, offering a rather limited benefit to the experience of notions like freedom and its natural boundaries.

Again and presumptuously, I gave this principle the value of a law and called it "the first law of law." As with all natural extracts interpreted by human reason, this law is deceptively simple at first glance but that ends right there, as we begin to peel the layers and examine their contents.

It follows that since this law was never before mentioned in the course of human history and for our purpose here, the first law of law states that:

Human personal and collective freedom, as an entity, ends, where the personal and collective freedom of another entity begins.

Of course, that is providing that our current notion of freedom is freshened up by the cultural instruments and perspectives presented here which are also natural extracts translated as best I can, into our cultural context.

Moreover, the first law of law upon arrival to the human cultural context at present has a long way to go before it can function in unison with nature, but again, it is a beginning. I'm saying that at first, its use by humanity will be largely within the species before its norms are extended to all other life.

In that sense freedom would be an open human prerogative to function in accordance to a survival strategy that brings a sufficiency of living so long as that sufficiency does not impede the same prerogative to another member of the same species.

In the overall sense of all life on Earth, freedom would be an open prerogative to function in accordance to a survival strategy that brings the individual and the species to which it belongs a sufficiency of living so long as that sufficiency does not impede the same prerogative to another species to also sustain their sufficiency.

The reason it is a first law of law is simply because all other laws can be derived or existing ones updated from this first law of law, using its substance as the guidelines for their sufficiency as laws.

The first law of law implies a norm in a perfect state of what scientists call symmetry, therefore when that symmetry is broken there are consequences. It is those consequences that are mediated by the laws derived from the first law of law.

As we set off on our migration, providing that we do, the first law of law, is an instrument that must be investigated, because the stability of the campaign against CEGE which surely is already with us, and whose severity, we have not really even acknowledged little else quantified even minimally, save in terms of climate change and global warming, agents that are tacitly acknowledged and even at that, the measures considered are mostly about what their impact would be to the economy and big business and the first people to be affected. Nothing much of significance about the rest of life, save for a few brave independent studies that do quite reasonably signal reasons for alarm and a need for corrective measures.

Anyway, greater simplicity in the understanding of the fundamental character of freedom and conduct, is as I said, vital to civilization entering the Anthropocene because the war against CEGE will be of long duration and improved conduct by the human population will prevent the social deterioration caused by the impacts of CEGE and the unnecessary drain of resources used, to appease tensions that can be better used to move forward.

To close up this book, I wish to emphasize that this book is a beginning too, it is a work of art, because the voice of art has always been the voice of change and transformation, if we know anything about our earliest history before the written word, it was art who provided the link between humanity and the world that we where learning to interpret.

This book is, in a real way, like the earliest cave paintings albeit with a narrative but not much different in essence, just as the cave paintings made as far back as 100,000 years ago signaled the start of symbolic thought and language, oddly enough not to far from the star of our migration out of Africa.

That was the symbolic language, which effectively inaugurated the long path to civilization with all of its attributes. Although symbols where never thought to have a direct effect in changing the world around us, we now know that they certainly had the power to change the way we perceive it and our capacity to change the world.

Data-A art and its aesthetic of unification with Nature and life itself, as its primary focus, has yielded a treasure trove of beginnings as mentioned here, but also a vision for our species and a world that is defined by and within the margins of Nature, a world where our power of intellect can see and carry-out the systematic realization of not only, most of the old promises and human ideals, but offer future generations the gift of life in a world where hope is a realizable notion, where peace is a daily reality and living is carried out with dignity and a measure of happiness for us and for the rest of life on earth.

We humanity, are a beautiful species that deserves to live at peace with ourselves and at peace with the world, let us not give up on a miracle that for some reason has come to us, in the form of a pair of nesting Osprey eagles whose offspring united art and life, as if to tell humanity that it is okay to evolve culturally and that it can be accomplished in friendship with the rest of the world.

"The End"

Epilogue

It has been a constant preoccupation of mine as I observe the world at present that this conversation may be late in starting as I see how nonchalantly nuclear warfare and the right to create and posses such weapons is spoken about lately as if the calamities that they entail were not already evident in history and blatantly visible through the Chernobyl and Fukushima nuclear affairs.

As the talk about revolution and resistance is brought onto the table fueled by the fatigue of just making a living by a public that is so fragmented that the idea of public is merely a relic of a once fairly cohesive society. Where corporate enterprise has been hijacked by CEGE, into an external entity to humanity that is taking control over the direction of the planet, with no regard for Nature or human life in the general sense, by which I mean, the proprietors, their administrators and everyone all the way down to the gate guard and those enabling its business plan in government.

As the devaluation of life outside of that interest has made the citizens of the world into spendable commodities, whose value, is assessed as units of labor and whose dignity as human beings is further curtailed by diminishing rights and social services that echo the days of open and accepted slavery.

These few points from a great many in the reality of our world today, are not points used to build a case against anyone, but they are critical issues to point at a grave mistake generated by the burden of an incomplete human cultural context, a context whose day of reckoning has come and whose rational response cannot be either ignored or denied, not without placing all of humanity and the planet at the disposition of CEGE.

What is frightening, is that CEGE, at the core of corporate enterprise, as the digital age has enabled it to be, reduces humanity to mere robots doing its bidding and like a cancer it will consume the host to the last, only to die with the host's demise.

Those concerns are at the crux of the Holocene legacy, but friends, we are not there anymore and in fact we could not return there even if we wanted to.

I think that the most important thing to look at, in this moment in history, is at the reality that shows us that we do not have to stay on a course where no body wins, the vision presented here may not be the perfect vision, but it is a vision we did not have before, it is a vision whose prospects are a lot more than just promises and much more than a good reason to have and offer hope for humankind.

The notion of a migration of the human mind is the only way to forever distance our species, from a cultural deficiency that was good while it lasted, but that now is the difference between survival and extinction.

We can do this together and really there is not a good reason not to try, as the other choice, extinction, is a choice that the culture, as is, has already made, we would just be reneging on a bad choice, to migrate out of it for the benefit of everyone on Earth. The rest is work and perseverance, it will take many generations to stabilize life on Earth but it is doable if we want.

Nature has still a lot of things to disclose to us about life, living and the survival strategies that enables life to do so. The Human nature-Nature partnership in the Anthropocene is not only key, but also the most formidable response we can afford.

Migration to other worlds may be an option for space exploration, but giving our record; who would want our kind at present, to populate other worlds just to repeat on them what we have done to ours.

We are a little late in getting started, however the job is still quite doable and a culture of world peace will afford us as good a stead as we can hope for; as we move forward.

How difficult can it possibly be, to take a deep breath, to hold the hands of those you love and allow life itself to lead our next great migration?

This is still home and we are still the smart species, we could not possibly have come this far just to go extinct with the satisfaction that we also killed all other life as our last stance of power.

With love and peace

Tiité Baquero

Acknowledgements

I have made mention of a number of people by name and used a few credited references I have done so because they are critical names to the relevance of the ideas they either created or are the best exponents at the moment. Therefore I thank them before hand for their contribution, as my intentions are solely to endow this work of art with the best possible relevant resources to the benefit of a cause that we are all trying to contribute to; life on earth. Anyone else who I missed and require to be credited will be credited in a subsequent edition with the proper apology.

Naturalist- Wendell Krull –page 37
Ecologist- Eugene F. Stoermer -page 46
Atmospheric chemist- Paul Crutzen –page 46
Christian Theologian- Saint Augustine- page 62
MIT researcher- Sheperd Doeleman –page 178
Veterinarian- Dr. Jesse R. White –page 208
Theoretical physicist- Albert Einstein –pages 172, 226, 235
Astronomer- Edwin Hubble –page 226
Cosmologist- Georges Lemaitre –page236
Theoretical Physicist- Stephen Hawking – page236
Mathematical physicist- Roger Penrose –page236
Art critic – Robert Hughes –page 264
Artist- Banksy –page 265
Artist- Ai Weiwei –page 265

List of Illustrations

The Habit of Migration
The Burden of War
Cognitive Bubble
Follow Life
CEGE
Art and Life Reconciled
Culture of Peace
Initial Conditions
The Proof
Cognitive Scape
Conscious Migration
Open Reality
In the Age of Life
A War for Life
Cultural Evolution
The Vision
First Law of Law
The End

All illustrations are from original works by the author and are intended to be the visual cue of each chapter, their combined effect, results in an art exhibit in book form, under the title "The Next Great Migration"

CPSIA information can be obtained
at www.ICGtesting.com
Printed in the USA
FSHW012002190820
73136FS